FREE AT LAST?

—The Tottenham Riots and the Legacy of Slavery

FREE AT LAST?

— The Tottenham Riots and the Legacy of Slavery

CLIFFORD HILL

Wilberforce Publications

First published in Great Britain in 2014 by
Wilberforce Publications Ltd
70 Wimpole Street, London W1G 8AX
All rights reserved.

Cover design by Carl Mapletoft

ISBN 978-0-9575725-2-2

Printed worldwide by Createspace
and in the UK by Imprint Digital, Exeter

Contents

Acknowledgments 10
Foreword 11
Preface 13

Chapter 1 **The Tottenham Riots of 2011** 21
1.1 In the Beginning
1.2 Parliament Recalled
1.3 Role of the Police
1.4 Public Confidence Damaged
1.5 Dysfunctional Families
1.6 Youth Anomie
1.7 Ethnic Composition of the Rioters
1.8 Soul-searching
1.9 Fatherless Families and Gangs
1.10 Family Breakdown

Chapter 2 **The Early Days** 33
2.1 Preparing the Ground
2.2 Culture Shock
2.3 Providing Employment
2.4 Record of Early Days
2.5 Accommodation Problems
2.6 Dealing with Disturbances
2.7 Partnership Schemes
2.8 Social Problems
2.9 Discipline
2.10 Opposition to Immigration
2.11 Powellism
2.12 Race Relations

Chapter 3 **Life in the Caribbean in 1962**   51

3.1   Visiting the West Indies
3.2   Slavery Taboo
3.3   Fears of Violence
3.4   The Slave Trade
3.5   'Going Home'
3.6   Family and Marriage
3.7   Common-Law Unions and the Role of Women
3.8   Sex and Pregnancy
3.9   Marriage
3.10   Colour Code and Social Class
3.11   Social and Cultural Norms
3.12   Generosity

Chapter 4 **Tottenham in the 1960s**   65

4.1   Life in Tottenham
4.2   Cold Comfort
4.3   Churches and Immigrants
4.4   Media Exposure
4.5   House Attacked
4.6   Reaction to Attack
4.7   Relationships with Other Churches
4.8   Culture Shock
4.9   Middle Class Institutions
4.10   Third Generation Theory
4.11   Pentecostals
4.12   Millennialist Message
4.13   Second Generation
4.14   Indictment of the Church

Chapter 5 **Third Generation Theory**   83

5.1   General Theory
5.2   First Generation Migrants
5.3   Second Generation Migrants
5.4   Third Generation Migrants
5.5   Summary
5.6   Additional Note
5.7   West Indian Migrants From 1948
5.8   African Migrants From 1950
5.9   Asian Migrants since 1960
5.10   The Problem Facing Parents

Chapter 6 **Colonial Slavery and the Trade Triangle**   99
6.1   Slave Ship Exhibition
6.2   Victims and Oppressors
6.3   US Constitution
6.4   Immigration Act 1596
6.5   Slavery Illegal in Britain
6.6   Abolition Campaign
6.7   Wilberforce
6.8   Trade Triangle
6.9   The Zong
6.10 Olaudah Equiano and Granville Sharp
6.11 Plantation Slavery
6.12 Loss of African Identity
6.13 End of Slavery

Chapter 7 **The Zong Project**   121
7.1   Finding a Replica Ship
7.2   The Royal Navy
7.3   The Slave Ship
7.4   Project Purpose
7.5   Painful Experience
7.6   Caribbeans
7.7   Anger and Reconciliation
7.8   Legacy of Slavery
7.9   Reconciliation
7.10 Key Findings of the Survey

Chapter 8 **White Slavery: 18th and 19th Century Britain**   135
8.1   Age of Revolution
8.2   White Slaves
8.3   Combination Acts
8.4   Children Exploited
8.5   Yorkshire Slavery
8.6   First Bill Presented
8.7   Factory Conditions
8.8   Ten Hour Act
8.9   Masters and Slaves Mentality
8.10 Chartist Movement
8.11 Violent Disorders
8.12 Trade Unions Emerge
8.13 Miners' Strike
8.14 Class War
8.15 'Plebgate'
8.16 Social Class Attitudes

Chapter 9 **Family and Culture Part 1**   157

9.1   Family Life in Jamaica — Household Types
9.2   Marriage
9.3   Sexual Relationships and 'Promiscuity'
9.4   Concubine Relationships
9.5   Fatherhood
9.6   Family Life among West Indian Immigrants in the UK
       in the 1950s and 1960s — Social Background
9.7   Immigration: a Political Issue
9.8   Immigration: a Social Issue
9.9   Family Life
9.10 Effects in the Caribbean
9.11 Struggle for Survival
9.12 Marriage and Common-Law Unions
9.13 Fatherhood
9.14 Youth

Chapter 10 **Family and Culture Part 2**   185

10.1   The Family in Britain from the 1950s
10.2   The Social Environment
10.3   The Social Conservatism of the 1950s
10.4   The Shock of the 1960s
10.5   The Era of Change
10.6   Results of the Social Revolution
10.7   Social Drivers behind the Revolution
10.8   The Arts and the Media
10.9   Fragmentation of Family Life
10.10 Background to the Riots

Chapter 11 **Social Inequality**   201

11.1   TUC Conference
11.2   Us and Them
11.3   White Slavery
11.4   Social Injustice
11.5   Colonial Slavery
11.6   Immigration
11.7   Social Darwinism
11.8   Racism
11.9   Police Injustice
11.10 Discrimination
11.11 Ongoing Injustice
11.12 The Churches
11.13 First Generation
11.14 Second Generation
11.15 Third Generation

Chapter 12 **Future Hope**   225

12.1   Legacy of Slavery
12.2   Caribbean Character
12.3   Nation-Building
12.4   Nelson Mandela
12.5   Tottenham
12.6   Betrayed
12.7   Pentecostals
12.8   Resilience and Determination
12.9   Children
12.10 Parents
12.11 Changing Society
12.12 Changing Lives
12.13 African Churches
12.14 An Illustration from History
12.15 The Spirit of Slavery
12.16 Thinking outside the Box
12.17 Breaking the Yoke
12.18 Community Development
12.19 Essential Developments
12.20 The Denominational Churches

Illustrations

1. Sunday evening worship in High Cross Church Tottenham — the largest multicultural congregation in London in the 1960s

2. High Cross Church on Commonwealth Sunday 1963 — the church was full and latecomers were unable to gain entry

3. The church house attacked by the BNP July 1963 with Council workmen turning over the paving stones to hide the offensive words NIGGER LOVER

4. The Zong slave ship moored in the Thames near Tower Pier during the 200th anniversary commemorations of the abolition of the slave trade, April 2007

ACKNOWLEDGEMENTS

I am very grateful to a number of my friends who have read the manuscript and made helpful comments. These include Dr Joe Aldred, The Revd Phyllis Thompson, The Revd Betty King, Pastor Tony Paul and Yemi Adedeji. I am grateful for those who proof-read the script for me in the early stages, particularly Neil Harvey and Paul Cadywould.

I want to thank John Scriven and Andrea Williams of Wilberforce Publications, for agreeing to publish the book but also for their help and encouragement. I am particularly grateful to Professor John Wolffe for his kindness not only in offering a number of helpful comments on the content but also for writing the Foreword to this book.

My own team at Issachar Ministries have been very supportive and especial thanks to John Matthews our chairman who has taken a particular interest in this book and greatly assisted in its production. The Ministry is committed to the concepts developed in this book and will be supportive of any positive outcome.

I am greatly indebted to my wife, Monica, who has not only participated in the writing and production of this book but has shared in the journey it represents, and given a lifetime of service to the communities of which we have jointly been privileged to belong.

This book is dedicated to our children, Jennifer, Alison and Stephen, who were born and raised in Tottenham and the East End of London; for their love, long-suffering and forgiveness in sharing their parents with the community in which we all lived and served.

Clifford Hill
January 2014

Foreword

John Wolffe
Professor of Religious History at the Open University

It is impossible to *change* the past. In this book, however, Clifford Hill points to many ways in which the manner in which we *view, interpret and reflect on* the past can have profound implications for the present and the future. Professional historians, such as myself, strive for objectivity and detachment, and in so doing we sometimes write books that, for all their erudition, appear irrelevant and inaccessible to people wrestling with contemporary problems.

Moreover, even we are not immune from our own more subtle kinds of bias, for example, as Clifford observes in Chapter 6, in giving disproportionate attention to the contribution of white people to the abolition of slavery, and insufficiently acknowledging the role of slaves and ex-slaves themselves. Politicians and other public figures often – sometimes unwittingly, sometimes unscrupulously – present distorted or selective readings of the past in order to serve the causes they are promoting in the present. Utterances of this kind have been very much in evidence in the aftermath of the riots of the summer of 2011 which are the starting point for the analysis in this book.

Clifford here draws both on his long experience of ministry in multi-ethnic communities in north and east London, and on his extensive knowledge of history and sociology to offer a distinctive and richly-informed assessment of the causes of the riots, and to set out his own vision for the future. He shows how the long shadow of slavery still blights relationships and perceptions. The arrival of numerous migrants from the Caribbean in England in the

1950s and 60s was initially a golden opportunity for historic reconciliation, but one that was missed as the endemic prejudices of British society and the churches engendered new phases of alienation and confrontation, with poisonous legacies that are still with us half a century later.

Nevertheless, there is hope for the future. In the past, white-led churches that 'froze out' black people were a major part of the problem, but the numerous dynamic black-led and genuinely multicultural churches which have grown up in recent decades have the potential to be part of the solution. If they are to do this, however, there needs to be a mature engagement with the past, acknowledging the pain and divisiveness rooted in racism and in black and white slavery, but also affirming the positive experiences and achievements of black people and the capacity of humankind to transcend historic separations of class, ethnicity and gender.

The 'Zong' project, described in Chapter 7, pioneered one way in which this can be done. Another complementary approach is offered by the 'Building on History: Religion in London' project I have recently been leading at The Open University (www.open.ac.uk/arts/religion-in-london), which seeks to provide tools to enable religious groups and their associated communities to engage constructively with their own histories.

All of us — whether academic or practitioner, black or white, African or Caribbean, Christian or secular — have much to learn from the insights offered in this book. We need to work together better to understand the past, to avoid perpetuating the mistakes that were made, to affirm the value of diverse cultural and religious heritages, and thereby to build a better future.

John Wolffe
October 2013

Preface

The legacy of slavery in the West Indian islands today and among those of Caribbean descent in Britain can be traced back to the days of unrest in the British Caribbean islands leading up to the Abolition of Slavery Act which was passed in London in 1833 and became effective on 1 August 1834. Not all slaves were released at that time as there was a five year period of apprenticeship, so that it was not until 1 August 1838 that all the African slaves were set free.

Abolitionist Campaign
For a number of years before the passing of the Abolition of Slavery Act, rumours of impending freedom had been circulating among the slave populations of all the islands. News of the abolitionist campaign in Britain was eagerly shared from plantation to plantation with increasing excitement and impatience. Since the abolition of the slave trade in 1807, missionaries had been sent to the West Indies in increasing numbers.

Particularly active were the Nonconformists of the London Missionary Society (Congregationalist), of which William Wilberforce was one of the founders in 1795, and the Baptist Missionary Society. Many of the planters welcomed these preachers in the hope that their teaching would counteract the power of *obeah* or folk religion in the slave quarters. Few plantations were without their local 'obeah' men, and the planters hoped that if the Africans became Christians they would cease playing their drums and dancing late into the night and become quieter and more docile.

Opposition to Education

There was considerable local opposition to the slaves being taught to read and write, but the missionaries prevailed on the grounds that it was essential for believers to be able to read the Bible for themselves. Their literacy, however, enabled them to read the news of the abolitionist campaign in London which indirectly led to an uprising of slaves in 1823 in the Demerara area of British Guiana. The Rev. John Smith was blamed for inciting this rebellion and was tried and sentenced to death. He died in prison three days before a royal pardon reached the colony, but his death gave considerable impetus to the abolition campaign in London, which had somewhat lost strength since the abolition of the trade.

From 1807 there were high expectations in Britain that when the planters were no longer able to purchase fresh supplies of labour from Africa this would lead to better treatment for the slaves, with improved standards of living and working conditions leading to more stable family life and child care.

> Instead, the islands were buffeted by disastrous revolts and ghastly repression. It seemed to more and more people that here was a system which was beyond repair or redemption; here were men — the planters — impervious to persuasion and unaware of human decency. To cap it all, they persecuted white missionaries and harassed black Christians.[1]

It was this brutal period and the subsequent terms of emancipation that were powerful influences in forming the mindset of African-Caribbean people which were to have lasting effect.

Brutality

The missionary-educated Africans in Jamaica eagerly followed news of the abolition campaign and, believing that they would assist the movement, some 60,000 slaves led by a local Baptist preacher, Samuel Sharpe, decided to go on strike in 1831. The strike was brutally repressed, with over 200 killed in the fighting and a massive 340 cruelly executed after being summarily tried. The missionaries were largely blamed by the planters and many of the chapels were destroyed, but the excessive violence and inhumanity of the authorities gave additional stimulus to the emancipation process in London and hastened the day of freedom for the slaves. Walvin's assessment was:

> It was as if the tables had been turned. Who now were the savages; who now the pagan, brutal people? In the years of emergent black Christianity, some of the most unchristian behaviour was to be found not in the slave quarters but in the Great House.[2]

Gross Injustice

Under the terms of the Abolition Act 1833, £20 million was paid to the owners of slaves in compensation for the loss of their 'property' but nothing at all to the freed Africans. It was widely expected that they would use their freedom to their own advantage in providing for themselves. Some chose to remain working on the sugar plantations as wage labourers, while others used the meagre savings they had obtained, through the sale of produce from the small strips of land they had been allowed for growing their own food, to obtain small parcels of land that could be worked as smallholdings. These were usually of poor quality soil but they formed the basis of the small peasant farming society that can still be seen in Jamaica today.

It seems surprising now that there was no public outcry at the gross injustice of compensating the slave owners but not the slaves. The abolitionists in Britain were, of course, 5,000 miles away from the West Indian islands and the exchange of news always involved a delay of several weeks. Abolitionists had to rely on the veracity of reports for their information, which often was grossly distorted to give a far more favourable impression of conditions among slaves than was factually true. Having won the political battle in London, the abolitionists felt that their job was done. In fact there was considerable pride in the achievement that had been won in the face of the massive political and economic power and influence of the planters.

Royal Navy

Attention in Britain from 1807, and especially after 1833, was turned into a kind of crusading zeal to end slavery throughout the world. In the period 1820–1870 the Royal Navy arrested some 1,600 ships on the high seas and freed more than 150,000 African slaves. This humanitarian zeal was not always purely motivated. There was a strong desire to stop the French from getting wealth and produce from their colonies and preventing the development of further American power while Britain was at war with both France and America.

Meanwhile the condition of the Africans in the Caribbean islands grew increasingly remote. It was no longer either a political or a moral issue. It was a battle that had been won and the British could add it to the mounting successes of the British Empire that rapidly became the pride of Victorian Britain. The Africans in the Caribbean islands had been set free. As far as the general population in Britain was concerned, the job was done. The islands soon faded out of public view. But the hardships faced by the former slaves, and the lack of resources, increased tensions throughout the populations of the islands.

Rebellion

In Jamaica these tensions spilled over into open rebellion at Morant Bay in October 1865, led by Paul Bogle, who organised a protest march to the courthouse, calling for justice. After ten days it was brutally repressed by the Government and by private militias employed by the planters. Nearly five hundred people were killed and an even larger number were flogged and brutally punished. Paul Bogle and George Gordon, whose only crime was to cry out for 'justice', were both hanged. Even as free men and women the people of Jamaica were still subjected to the unrestrained cruelty of their overlords.

Heroes' Day

In an inspiring message to the nation on Heroes' Day on 22 October 2013, the Most Honourable Portia Simpson Miller, Prime Minister of Jamaica, urged her fellow-Jamaicans to study their history and be proud of their heroes who had self-sacrificially struggled for justice and freedom. She said: "In celebrating the theme, 'Our History...Our Strength', we must draw on the history of selfless national service given by our heroes, their history of putting the interests of others ahead of themselves— indeed, risking their lives for others. Fellow Jamaicans, we need more than ever to recapture that spirit at every level in this country." She ended by quoting Marcus Garvey: "A people without knowledge of their past history, origin and culture is like a tree without roots."

Britain Today

Many young people in inner-city areas in the great cities of Britain have little or no knowledge of their history. Black young people of West Indian origins are unable to trace their African roots, which were cut off by colonial slavery.

For many white young people, the tragedy of dysfunctional family life means that they are unable even to know their own father. As a simple matter of justice, the plight of a million unemployed young people growing up in a situation of hopelessness and despair should weigh heavily upon the conscience of the nation, which ought to lead to radical measures of social change. Sadly, we see very little awareness and understanding of the situation among our politicians.

The Prime Minister, David Cameron, initially dismissed the Tottenham riots as "sickening criminality" although he later declared the Government's intention of improving the lives of the most dysfunctional families. But little or nothing appears to have been done since the riots. In London, some £3 million a year is being spent on encouraging social enterprise projects among young people involved in gangs, with the object of weaning them away from gang life. But these are all tinkering around the edges and not tackling the central problems of the ghettoisation of poverty and deprivation among the inner-city underclass.

Root Causes
In this book we attempt to analyse the root causes of the social malaise that envelops inner-city life for some four million households. The research upon which this book is based covers a legacy of slavery that affects both black and white young people in inner-city areas. It is a hangover from the injustice and cruelty of what William Wilberforce in the eighteenth century described as 'white slavery' among the victims of the Industrial Revolution in Britain and 'colonial slavery' among the Africans who were transported three thousand miles across the Atlantic to a life of forced servitude in British colonial territories.

History has drawn a veil over these atrocities for more

than two hundred years and it is time to strip away that veil of secrecy and reveal the truth. In so doing there is a chance that the conscience of the nation may be stirred in a similar manner to that which resulted in the abolition of the slave trade in 1807, when Wilberforce pleaded with the nation to renounce the inhumanity and injustice of policies that were driven by greed and self-interest. His plea was for a policy that would "make goodness fashionable". That is the plea echoed in this book.

Investment

It is time to say to the people of Jamaica, Barbados, Trinidad and other former British colonies how deeply we regret the three-hundred-year period during which our forefathers practised the unspeakable horrors of slavery, and to do whatever we can to encourage investment in social enterprise projects and other economic measures that will benefit those who are struggling with poverty and under-development that are part and parcel of the legacy of slavery. With regard to young people in Britain's inner-city areas, both black and white, we need to discover imaginative and creative ways of enabling them to develop their skills and abilities, and to exercise them in a caring social environment. It is surely not beyond the wit of human beings in this advanced technological age to ensure that its wealth and resources are used for this purpose.

Clifford Hill
January 2014

Notes

[1] James Walvin, *Black Ivory*, Blackwell, London, 2002, p. 264.

[2] *Ibid*.

Chapter One

THE TOTTENHAM RIOTS OF 2011

1.1 In the Beginning

The shooting dead by police of a young man from the West Indian community in the Broadwater Farm area of Tottenham, North London, in August 2011 sparked the worst communal disturbances seen in Britain for half a century. He was a passenger in a minicab, and although a loaded handgun was found in his possession it had not been fired when he was shot by police marksmen. Shortly before this he had sent a text to his girlfriend saying that he was being tailed. News of the shooting, and the lack of any information supplied by the police, upset his family. Two days later, on Saturday afternoon 6 August 2011, they organised a small community march to the local police station in Tottenham High Road, seeking information. They were left standing in the street. No senior police officer came to address them.

This led to a much larger demonstration that evening which sparked three nights of chaos in London, where gangs of hooded youths indulged in indiscriminate looting and arson. London was quieter on Tuesday night after 16,000 police officers, the biggest deployment in UK history, were sent onto the streets. But copycat violence had already erupted in other parts of London, such as Croydon and Hackney. Older residents in Croydon remembered the Second World War and likened the torching of the 'House of

Reeves' furniture store to the wartime bombing. City areas around the country, particularly Manchester, Birmingham, Liverpool and Bristol were also affected.

The torching of 'Carpetright' in Tottenham caused considerable local resentment, not simply because the firm were known to have put a lot of money into charitable work in the community, but because there were a number of flats above the shops and people's lives were put at risk. Many residents and small business owners lost everything in the fire. The riots also led to a community response in a number of areas, with local residents turning out in force with brooms to sweep the streets and clear the rubbish away from their neighbourhoods. An editorial in *The Times* noted that these good citizens were 'mainly middle class'.

1.2 Parliament Recalled

The Prime Minister cut short his holiday, returned to Britain and recalled Parliament. He strongly condemned the "sickening criminality" which had caused some £100 million of damage, and he said that those responsible would "feel the full force of the law". This soon became clear as the police began screening large quantities of CCTV footage and arresting identified culprits.

The one-day sitting of Parliament brought strong condemnation of the riots from all sides of the House of Commons. It also sparked a national debate on the root causes of the disturbances that involved large numbers of children and young people in destructive criminal acts. The immediate result was a sharp disagreement between senior members of the Government and the police. MPs criticised the police for their failure to act immediately in quelling the riotous behaviour in Tottenham that led to extensive looting of premises, with many reports of police standing by and watching rather than moving in and arresting the offenders.

1.3 Role of the Police

Newspaper reports said that people were stunned by the spectacle of riot police standing by while mobs cleaned out and torched shops and businesses — scenes that were witnessed by millions on British television news and repeated in other countries right across the world. This was an international humiliation for a nation that has always prided itself upon its law and order. It appeared that the police were slow to respond, which allowed the riots to spread. It was reported that the police treated the original disturbances as 'public order offences' rather than criminal activity, and they were unprepared for the scale and seriousness of the disturbances. It was not until the Prime Minister returned to the country that the capital was flooded with police officers, which gave politicians the opportunity to say that it was they, rather than the police, who controlled the situation.

The police retaliated by saying that if they had 'gone in hard' on the first night of the disturbances they would have been accused of overreacting and spoiling decades of hard work in improving community relationships. Many police officers were depressed by not only having to face large hostile crowds armed with bricks and petrol bombs, but also having to suffer criticism of their methods. They had previously been criticised for hard tactics such as 'kettling' in dealing with mobs at previous demonstrations, and now they were accused of being too soft. A spokesman for the Metropolitan Police said, "It is much better to watch video and contain than to order running battles which would put lives at risk." Some three thousand arrests were subsequently made, which resulted in many custodial sentences that overfilled the prisons and caused a public outcry that sentencing had been too severe, especially in relation to first-time offenders and children.

1.4 Public Confidence Damaged

These widespread disorders shocked the nation for their violence, looting, arson, and the scale of destruction. There were calls for the use of plastic bullets, tear gas and water cannon, but others said that the police were not to blame — it was the politically correct politicians who restricted the use of force under all circumstances, insisting on 'softly softly' tactics. If they used force on offenders the police were afraid that they would subsequently be faced with court proceedings which would damage their careers.

The most serious damage was done to public confidence in the institutions of state as these instances of rioting occurred hard on the heels of the banking crisis, the mounting national debt, chaos on the stock market, the scandal of MPs' allowances and expenses, and the phone hacking scandal. If even the police could not be trusted to guard the nation, the sky was indeed falling in.

Many commentators feared that the kind of scenes we had been witnessing on the streets of Middle Eastern cities through what had become known as the 'Arab Spring' would spread to Britain. It was recognised that the same social media that had played a large part in bringing down the Egyptian Government and aiding rebellion against repressive regimes had also played a large part in encouraging young people to participate in the looting and destruction that had occurred in British cities. But, in addition, many perceptive observers of the social scene were looking for the roots of the troubles that caused young people to take to the streets.

1.5 Dysfunctional Families

David Cameron returned to his pre-election theme of 'Broken Britain' and declared his intention[1] of transforming the lives of the 120,000 most dysfunctional families by the year 2015. Other commentators said that it was not just a handful of families who were responsible for the troubles in our inner cities, but we were a nation whose moral values were collapsing. They pointed to the evidence that secular humanists, who have exercised influence in both Labour and Conservative governments, have deliberately undermined traditional values to promote their own so-called equality agendas that have undermined marriage and family values. They have produced a generation of parents and teachers who are either unable or unwilling to teach children the basic difference between right and wrong. We are now two generations away from those who were taught biblically-based Christian values that had been the foundation for the nation.

This theme was pursued by a number of right-wing newspapers. Max Hastings, in *The Daily Mail*,[2] said that we should be blaming the liberal orthodoxy that denies members of the underclass the discipline they need, while giving them a sense of entitlement that exacts no penalty for abusive behaviour. He said that the results were – "My dogs are better behaved and subscribe to a higher code of values than the young rioters in Hackney." Philip Johnston, in *The Daily Telegraph*,[3] said that millions have been spent trying to regenerate rundown areas so that it is nonsense to blame Government cuts and poverty for the behaviour of the rioters.

1.6 Youth Anomie

By contrast, Stafford Scott, in *The Guardian*,[4] after express-ing his horror for the 'mindless violence', made no mention of the mixed races involved in the riots but said that the reason why black youths seem unfazed about burning down their own neighbourhood is because they feel they have no stake in it. He said that they had grown up without fathers on estates where the few who do work are on miserable wages. Having forsaken all hope of attainment in the white man's world, they find support and a sense of community in the gang. He said that there were twenty-two gangs in Hackney alone. Most of them are involved in the drugs scene, which is what 'brings in the money'. *The Independent* said that it is the mindset of the gangs to, '... steal, riot and generally kick against authority.'[5] This lay behind the scenes we had witnessed, which were: 'a conflagration of aggression from a socially and economically excluded underclass'.

A different view was expressed by Matthew Syed, in *The Times*,[6] who said that the simple explanation is that young people who are bored with life do it for the sheer thrill of it all. He said that if you listen on the mobile phones to the giggles that accompany the window smashing, you see that among a minority of young males, regardless of race, the whiff of anarchy, the smashing up of places, and the harassing of respectable people is precisely what they seek out of life. It's invigorating.

1.7 Ethnic Composition of the Rioters

It is important to note the ethnic composition of the rioters which shows that this was not a race riot. The Ministry of Justice published a report in February 2012, giving the demographic statistics of those charged with participating in the riots up to 1 February 2012. This revealed the following statistics relating to those brought before the courts:

- 41% identified themselves as from the White Group
- 39% from the Black Group
- 12% from the Mixed Ethnic Group
- 6% from the Asian Ethnic Group
- 2% from Other Ethnic Groups.

The figures for the London Borough of Haringey, which includes Tottenham, showed that 55% of those brought before the courts were black, compared to the local population which at that time was 17% black. It is also significant that the overwhelming majority of those in the Black Group were of West Indian extraction and very few came from Africa. A further interesting statistic was that 90% of those involved in the riots were males; 26% were aged between 10–17; 27% were aged 18–20, and only 5% were over 40 years of age.

1.8 Soul-searching

All this was just the beginning of a prolonged period of national soul-searching, trying to discover the reason why the riots, the looting and the violent destruction should have spontaneously engulfed so many different areas. This attempt to understand the problem was sharpened by the knowledge that the scenes of mayhem had been transmitted around the world, which was not only damaging to British self-esteem but could have also damaged the prospects of the 2012 London Olympics. The harsh retributive justice handed down to many of the children and young adults engaged in the disturbances was no doubt partly with this in mind, and with a concern to show that this kind of behaviour would not be tolerated and was unlikely to occur again.

If there was any consensus in regard to the cause of the disturbances, it was undeniable that the majority of those involved came from some of the most economically and socially deprived areas in Britain. It was also notable that the objectives of the looters were primarily to steal fashion goods and clothes, including sportswear, as well as digital devices, iPads and mobile phones, personal computers, laptops and other electrical equipment. These are all things that the celebrity culture flaunts, the advertising industry powerfully portrays, and which are highly desirable among young people. If an opportunity to acquire such desirable goods without cost is presented to marginalised young people with little prospect of wealth, they will seize it, especially if they are living in a society that has long since abandoned any semblance of a work ethic, and one in which traditional family life is non-existent for many of its children.

1.9 Fatherless Families and Gangs

In any search for the roots or underlying social issues that triggered the widespread disturbances, we have to look at the communities from which most of those who actively participated come. The major characteristic is dysfunctional family life. Family breakdown, reconstituted families, fatherlessness, unemployment and chaotic home life are the background and daily life experience of many young people in inner-city areas. Undoubtedly, this kind of home life is a major factor influencing the behaviour of young people brought up in such conditions, and the gangs they join are a substitute for stable family life.

The gang gives identity and security, two things most needed for survival in the inner-city. The major things that gangs cannot give are love, comfort and compassion. The gang imposes its own rules and has its own methods of discipline, but its rules of behaviour are those of an under-class rather than those that are acceptable in wider society. They have in-group norms that are socially acceptable within the gang but produce what society regards as deviant behaviour.

In the immediate aftermath of the disturbances that began in Tottenham, there were many references to the role played by the gangs. David Cameron promised to declare war on the gangs, but gang life is an outcome of a deeper social malaise. For politicians who have never lived in inner-city areas to condemn the gangs is to miss the target — it is looking in the wrong direction, at the outcome or by-product of the real issues.

1.10 Family Breakdown

There were numerous comments by politicians giving their views on the reasons for the riots, including a contribution by Iain Duncan Smith, the Work and Pensions Secretary. Writing in *The Times*,[7] he said that society had turned a blind eye to the festering problems shared by four million households across England. He said that, "For years now, too many people have remained unaware of the true nature of life on some of our estates." This was because we had ghettoised many of these problems, keeping them out of sight of the middle class majority. But last month the inner-city finally came to call, and the country was shocked by what it saw. He referred to the crumbling of moral values in the nation, saying: "The distorted morality has permeated our whole society, right to the very top. Whether in the banking crisis, phone hacking, or the MPs' expenses scandal, we have seen a failure of responsibility from the leaders in our society."

Since the early 1960s, family life in Britain has been slowly eroded by the forces of social change which have been closely associated with a liberal, secular/humanist agenda that has gained increasing political influence in all three political parties. They have influenced policy in both Labour and Conservative Governments, and were particularly active in the 'New Labour' government of Tony Blair that initiated social reforms emanating from the so-called 'equality' agenda. These measures gave further impetus to the social forces undermining marriage and stable family life, with the inevitable results that we have seen on the streets of Tottenham and in many other inner-city areas. Once the family, defined by Jack Straw when he was Home Secretary in 1998 as the 'building block of society', begins to crumble, the foundations of the nation are shaken. These were just some of the views and comments of politicians and social commentators given in the media.

Some commentators compared the riots with previous outbreaks of communal violence such as Broadwater Farm in 1985 and Notting Hill in 1958. The major difference was that these earlier riots, particularly the Notting Hill disturbances, were racial. They were confrontations between black and white youths, whereas in the 2011 riots, including Tottenham High Road where the disturbances began, black and white young people joined together against the police in destroying property and looting. The same pattern was repeated in Hackney and Croydon and other inner-city areas. The riots were certainly not racial and appeared to be largely an expression of disaffected urban youth.

But why did a small incident involving one family develop so rapidly into major communal disturbances with widespread destruction of property and causing danger to life? Why was it that an incident in one part of London should spark similar violent disturbances in other parts of London and copycat action in other cities? Why was it that young people of different racial origins should spontaneously join together in destroying property in their neighbourhood? Clearly this was not simply about supporting a family who were having problems in getting information from the police about the death of a relative. What are the roots of the social situation that gave rise to the Tottenham riots? What is the outlook for the future? Are there any real signs of hope?

These are the questions we must examine.

POSTSCRIPT

The verdict of the inquest into the death of 29-year-old Mark Duggan was that the police had lawfully killed him. The verdict of the jury provoked a violent outburst in the courtroom from the Duggan family who declared that the jury had colluded in the execution of Mark in face of the evidence that he was unarmed at the time of his death.

A gun had been found some 10 feet away from his body behind a fence from which it had been concluded that he had flung it away when his taxi was stopped by the police in Tottenham. The Duggan family and their supporters chanted outside the court "No justice, no peace". The reaction to this inquest which did not come until January 2014, nearly 2½ years after the shooting, shows that the tensions in the community remain today and add to the significance of the subject examined in this book.

Notes

[1] David Cameron, reported in *The Guardian*, 16 August 2011.

[2] *Daily Mail*, Max Hastings, 12 August 2011.

[3] *The Daily Telegraph*, 16 August 2011.

[4] *The Guardian*, Stafford Scott, 16 October 2011.

[5] *The Independent* Monday, 8 August 2011.

[6] *The Times*, Matthew Syed, 8 August 2011.

[7] *The Times*, Iain Duncan Smith, 15 September, 2011.

Chapter Two

THE EARLY DAYS

2.1 Preparing the Ground

My experience of working among immigrants from the Caribbean had begun in a purely fortuitous and unplanned manner. I arrived in Harlesden, west London, in 1952 as the newly ordained minister of Harlesden Congregational Church. I came straight from theological college, bright-eyed and innocent, with no experience of inner-city life. Although originally from east London, most of my boyhood and adolescence had been spent in the salubrious suburb of North Ruislip, Middlesex, where my family home backed into woodland through which I could walk to the Ruislip Lido or the Northwood golf course, where I spent many an idle hour. It was an idyllic setting. So I was almost totally unprepared for the task ahead of me. My university education and my theological studies had given me a good grounding in ancient Greek and the Classics, which were virtually useless in coping with my new responsibilities. Although I had taken a course in sociology as an additional subject, I had little understanding of the way the structures of society actually worked, and even less of the peculiar problems I would encounter.

I knew nothing of life in the West Indian islands, which were home to the one or two black people in my congregation, but they had a strange attraction for me. I soon began visiting them and talking about their experiences since coming to London. My learning curve was steep and I soon found that the problems they were encountering were very different from those of the white members of my church. Most of them were living in overcrowded conditions in large rundown Victorian houses which had been adapted for multiple-family living with varying degrees of success. The problems of accommodation were to become a major part of my life in the coming years. I myself lived in a seven bedroom church house on three floors on the Harrow Road with a brass plaque outside announcing that it was 'The Manse', making it a magnet for every passing tramp in west London. I was unmarried at the time but my parents had self-sacrificially left their house in Ruislip to keep home for me.

2.2 Culture Shock

I was suddenly plunged into the unfamiliar environment of an urban industrial population that was going through the upheavals of massive social change due to the large number of West Indian immigrants settling in the area and many white families moving out to the suburbs. This was having an unsettling effect upon those who either did not have the economic ability to move out or the personal security to take the risk of leaving the familiar landscape of the decaying inner-city milieu into which they had been born. The newcomers were already making a social impact, not only through their visible presence, but through their behaviour, closely observed by their white neighbours.

I can still vividly remember my own sense of shock when, within days of my arrival, a young West Indian couple came to me to book a wedding, and when I had taken note of all their details and fixed the date for the ceremony, they showed no inclination to go but clearly had something else on their minds. At last the girl said, "And whilst we are here, Parson, we'd like to book the christening." I made some foolish remark to the effect that this was rather anticipating a happy event. They looked puzzled for a moment and then she said, "Well, we'd like to get the date booked because he's already three months old."

My middle class English mores took a nosedive! In early 1950s England, living together before marriage was virtually unheard of, and illegitimacy was a social sin that brought disgrace upon the whole family and lowered the tone of the neighbourhood. I had much to learn! But it was this recognition of the inadequacies of my academic background and training for the work I felt called to do, that eventually led me to register in London University as a postgraduate student, to read for a doctorate in sociology. I knew this was going to be hard, with the many practical demands that were already being made upon my time, but I knew it was necessary.

By contrast to the first couple, within a few weeks another West Indian young couple came asking to be married, and I discovered that the bride-to-be had been an evangelist in Jamaica with the New Testament Church of God. It was my first encounter with Pentecostals, of whom I knew nothing except what I had learned in a course on twentieth century church history. I had never actually met a Pentecostal before —not even a white one! The bride and groom were not living together, and it appeared that the Pentecostals had a different set of social values, more akin to the English values with which I and my church members were familiar. The church soon took this young couple to heart and decided, as a wedding present, to give them the reception, which was arranged in the church hall.

This was a great community occasion as white and 'coloured'[1] Christians rejoiced together. After the more formal part of the reception there was an informal party. Our

young people soon had the Jamaicans joining enthusiastically in square dancing and, in their turn, some of their guests
showed the white people dances and music that delighted
our teenagers.[2] Their week's honeymoon was spent at the
Manse, after which they returned to their one room on the
third floor of a large house in Kilburn, which was literally
full of coloured families.

I was always grateful for the week that they spent in my
home, during which I was privileged to enter closely into
the lives of two fellow-Christians. I learned much of their
customs and way of life as they spoke about their background
in a Jamaican township and their church. All this was to
prove immensely useful in my future ministry.

2.3 Providing Employment

It was not only problems of accommodation that occupied
much of my time in those early days of working among
migrants from the West Indies. Helping them to find suitable
employment took a lot of my time. In fact, the Manse
became locally known as 'the Jamaican labour exchange'.
It was during the hard winter of 1954 that it really earned
this reputation. The weather was bitterly cold and jobs were
scarce. Every day brought fresh tales of despair as sometimes
six men at one time would crowd into my tiny study for help
in seeking work and somewhere to live. Each boat brought
hundreds more to swell the queues at the employment
exchanges, and with each reported landing with pictures
in the newspapers, I knew that it would not be many days
before I would be talking to some of the migrants in my
study. With each individual I would go through a regular
routine of questions, and in time I became quite experienced
at 'screening' them and placing them in suitable jobs.
I would scan the employment columns of local newspapers
and build up a list of employers who were willing to take

on coloured labour. Some employers would not engage them on principle. A few others excused themselves on the ground that they feared trouble, either from the unions, or from their English employees. On the whole, the majority of employers received my enquiries kindly and proved willing to take on suitable men if they had vacancies. It was a time when the post-war economy was booming and there was a considerable demand, especially for unskilled or semi-skilled labour. Several firms became regular customers in my 'labour market'. Their personnel managers used to telephone the Manse, describe their job vacancy and ask for a suitable man. I had all the particulars of background and education of each one and would send the most suitable.

All these firms spoke of the dependability of the Jamaican worker once they had completed a period of training and aculturalisation. One firm in Wembley would only take coloured workers if they came from me. They said that the Labour Exchange clerical staff had no experience of dealing with immigrants and did not understand them. So I had the strange experience of having a number of Jamaicans call and say that they had applied for a job there, but were told that they could not be considered unless they had a letter from me!

2.4 Record of Early Days
It was a sad fact of life that the kind of job many were able to get required them to do unsociable hours, including Sunday work. For the more committed Christians Sunday work was anathema as the following letter reveals.

Dear Minister,

Please accept usual greetings in Jesus' Sweet and Holy Name. Sir, I am indeed sorry to know that I never had the privilege yesterday evening to come to Service, through having to go to work. Only the dear Lord knows my feeling toward that. Anyway, I truly know by the Grace of God, he is going to open a way for me that I shall be able to go to church more often. I could remember Sundays back home, preaching to hundreds of people. I thank you very much, Sir, for that love and mercy you have for us the coloured. God bless you, and I know that the Dear Lord, will reward you. I believe, by God's grace I will be there Sunday evening at church, and I'm trying to bring some friends along with me. Please remember me in your prayers. I am yours in the Master's service.[3]

I received lots of little notes like this, some of which I preserved as a precious record of the early days of working among those whom I came to love and respect. They, on their part, freely expressed their gratitude for any help that I was able to give them. Typical of many such letters is the following:

To My Dear Minister,

Please accept warmest Christian Greetings in the Sweet Name of Jesus Christ, our soon coming King of Glory. Dear Sir, it gives me great joy to send you these few lines, giving you thanks for the nice job which the Dear Lord help you to get for me. Well, I must say you have done more for me than my mother could. As I came in from work, I had to kneel and pray for you that God may bless you more and give you the best of health to do his work, and then at last, according to Revelation 20:6, you may reign with him a thousand years. May the Lord ever Bless you and keep you in His Love, till He come. Please give your mother and father my greetings.

Yours in His Love and Grace[4]

In the early days of the migration during the 1950s there was a strong sense of community among the early settlers from the Caribbean. Many of them were ex-servicemen who had served with the British Army during the Second World War. They had experienced conditions in Britain at first hand and they had pleasant memories of a warm and friendly reception. On returning home they found high unemployment and were unable to settle, so they used their savings to buy a one-way passage to Britain, usually about £80. Others had spent a few years of employment in the USA, where they had earned sufficient money to enable them to save for emigration to Britain. Under US law, a West Indian could not settle and could only work for a limited period after which his visa would not be renewed.

2.5 Accommodation Problems

Upon reaching England, the first two requirements were to find employment and accommodation. The areas of settlement in London were already crowded, and finding a room to rent was not easy. Local newspapers and shop window advertisements openly displayed the prejudice of local property owners. It was quite usual to see notices displaying the words 'No Coloured' or more politely, 'Sorry, No Coloured' – indicating that the advertiser, at least, was aware that they were doing something which was morally wrong! This was little comfort to the new migrant who was desperate for somewhere to live. No help was given to them from any official quarters and there were no advisory centres to help newcomers to cope with their new surroundings or to deal with the practical problems of living in London or any other big city, which were very real and very strange for those who came from rural tropical areas, especially for those who came in midwinter!

Out of sheer necessity the early migrants began to solve their own accommodation problems by buying houses and letting rooms to their fellow countrymen. Most of these were run down, dilapidated and poorly maintained properties. In many cases they were sold with sitting tenants in part of the premises and this became a major bone of contention in race and community relationships. The sitting tenants were usually elderly white residents who had lived in the area for many years. They had no desire to move, and the new Caribbean owner often did not know British housing law and that sitting tenants were protected. They had bought in good faith, and when the white tenant refused to go and the new owner was unable to get the help of the law, they sometimes resorted to tactics that made life unbearable for the elderly residents who simply wanted a quiet life and could not cope with loud music blaring day and night. Some landlords deliberately used these tactics to try to persuade unwanted tenants to move, particularly if they were paying low rents that could not be revised due to legal protection.

2.6 Dealing with Disturbances

I was often called to deal with local disturbances and to settle disputes of this nature which were threatening to involve the whole street. On more than one occasion the local police rang me during the early hours of the morning and asked me to come to quieten things down. If they went into the house where the beer was flowing freely and rocksteady off-beat music[5] was throbbing through the night air, it was almost certain that there would be physical resistance and arrests which could trigger ethnic unrest. I would get dressed and drive as quickly as possible to the address they gave. I would immediately enter the house, knowing that the sight of my clerical collar would protect me, as even the inebriated would respect my office. I would speak to the miscreants and usually within a very short time the whole household would settle down.

I covered quite a large area of west London around Paddington, Queen's Park and Notting Hill. Inevitably there was damage to local community relationships by these disturbances. It was incidents like this that multiplied in Notting Hill and which triggered the 1958 riots involving the community on both sides of the ethnic divide. Once they began, disaffected residents came from different areas around London to join in the disturbances, in much the same way as they did in Tottenham in 2011 more than fifty years later.

Stuart Hall, a Birmingham University lecturer, himself a West Indian immigrant, wrote a booklet in 1967 looking back on this period. It was published by the National Committee for Commonwealth Immigrants, of which I was a member. The booklet dealt with the subject of young people in the immigrant communities. He recorded his own experience of Notting Hill:

> During the troubles in Notting Hill in 1958, I was teaching at a secondary school in a poor area of London, which was also, typically, an area of high migration. Several of the (white) boys in my class had participated in the incidents and we frequently discussed this in the classroom. An interesting fact about the discussions was that the boys held two quite separate and contradictory ideas. On the one hand they believed (often repeating the casual conversation of their parents) that West Indians were savages flooding the country, taking jobs, filling up classrooms, stealing women; that they were a lower order of society altogether and should be encouraged to 'go home'.
>
> On the other hand, they had the friendliest of attitudes towards me (a teacher who, after all, had 'stolen' a job in their school) and their own West Indian classmates (a group clearly 'filling up the classrooms'). To these boys, I and the other West Indians they knew were persons, individuals. It was impossible for them to maintain their hostility in the face of personal, day-to-day contact. But the West Indians in

Notting Hill were 'a group', 'them', outsiders, and unknowns. There appeared to be very little carry-over from the intimate and personal situation of the classroom to the impersonal situation on the streets of North Kensington.[6]

2.7 Partnership Schemes

From 1953 to 1958 I wrote a weekly column for a syndicate of west London newspapers, which included the Willesden Chronicle and the Kilburn Times. I was often asked to speak to meetings of various organisations such as rotary clubs and civic meetings. One of the questions that invariably came from white people in the audience was how was it that West Indians who came as economic refugees in search of work were able to afford to buy houses and to become landlords? The answer was that they did it through what was then known as a 'Partnership Scheme'. These schemes were operated by any number of West Indians who either had ties of kinship or who came from the same area in one of the islands. They lived together, worked together or lived in the same vicinity. The groups usually numbered between six and thirty, although some were even larger than this. One member of the group was appointed banker. It was his task to collect a certain fixed sum of money, maybe as little as one pound, from each member of the group, every weekend. Having collected all the contributions, he then paid out the whole sum to one member of the group. He had a list of names of all those in the group and they took turns to receive the whole amount. I described the way this scheme worked in *Black and White in Harmony* which was published at the time of the 1958 Notting Hill riots.

One of the members of my church was in a 'Partner Group' consisting of thirty West Indians, each of whom paid two pounds per week to the 'community bank', and each of whom then received sixty pounds every thirty weeks. My

Jamaican friend purchased a house in conjunction with a friend of his who also attended my church. They were in need of money for furniture as well as for the deposit on the house. He therefore arranged to purchase the house the week when it was his turn to receive sixty pounds. He also arranged with members of the group that his friend should be the first on the new rota, so that he would receive the sixty pounds the following week. Thus they received £120 within seven days, which gave them sufficient for the deposit on the house as well as for furniture. This was quite a common practice among partner groups, and this is the way in which they helped one another when there was a particular need. Any 'partner' could arrange to draw the amount of money that had been paid in, plus an advance of a similar sum, within seven days. The scheme operated quite successfully, although it depended entirely upon mutual trust and the honouring of promises.[7]

This was the way many of the migrants in the 1950s and 60s became landlords, which was a mystery to the local white population and a source of annoyance and jealousy, especially among older residents who had been left behind when the more affluent whites had moved out of the area to more salubrious suburbs when the immigrants began moving in.

2.8 Social Problems

In a perceptive passage, Stuart Hall offered an analysis of some of the social tensions in the areas of immigrant settlement. He wrote:

These are the areas for the socially dispossessed. Coloured immigrants are only one dispossessed social group crowding into these urban ghettos. Coloured immigrants in these areas encounter multiple hostilities. They are suspiciously regarded simply because they are coloured and foreign; because they don't fit the mental and cultural landscape and, doubly so, because they are judged from the pressured position of native families already under severe social stress. The British families condemned to the 'twilight zones' are only too conscious of others who are doing well. They fear a further decline in their status — already a fragile position; fear competition for scarce jobs, scarce housing, scarce school places and welfare provision. They believe that the influx of yet another group will bring the few remaining barriers they have erected between themselves and social dislocation crumbling down.[8]

Hall added:

Paradoxically, immigrant families believe English parents are too lax and too indulgent with their children, too slovenly about the house. They feel that they are keeping up standards which 'the natives' around them are rapidly abandoning. Such misconceptions never meet — they coexist. There is no-one — except the young immigrant, who is the busiest traveller between the two hostile worlds — to 'translate' between the groups. Each stands solidly behind reinforced barricades. And the person most affected by these barricades is the young immigrant. He has to learn to negotiate the hostility of both groups; to cope with the suspicion of his alien environment— neighbours, school friends, workmates and the police. But he also has to negotiate the fears of his own family and the determination of his parents that, at whatever cost, their dignity will not be lowered; their children will not fraternise too freely lest they be thought 'pushing'; their girls will not stay out late lest they be thought loose; their boys will not expose themselves to situations in which they may be rebuffed and rejected.[9]

2.9 Discipline

The first generation of immigrants from the West Indies exercised strict discipline with their children. Family life was well ordered and there was considerable pride in maintaining a good name. If one of the children was arrested for some offence it brought disgrace upon the whole family and such an event was to be avoided at all costs, hence the strict discipline which was enforced within the family. This discipline often involved quite severe physical punishment, such as was common in chastising children in family life in all the West Indian islands.

This discipline was often a cause of deep resentment among the children of immigrants, especially those born in this country who grew up with a predominantly white peer group. They were keen to be accepted by their school friends and they noticed that discipline within the homes of white children was considerably less strict than in their homes. At the same time, discipline within schools in Britain began to be more relaxed as new methods of education came through a new generation of post-war educationalists and teachers. Social mores of the second-generation immigrants began to change, but so too did those of their parents under the impact of the stresses and strains of life in the immigrant communities. It is here that we are able to trace the beginnings of the social situation that exists in present-day Tottenham and many other similar urban environments.

2.10 Opposition to Immigration

Stuart Hall was lamenting in the mid-1960s that his hopes of full integration into the host community in the early days of the migration to Britain had not materialised and seemed to be farther away with each new experience of rejection, such as was represented by the Notting Hill riots and the bitter debate that took place prior to the passing of legislation limiting immigration in 1962. This debate was not only in Parliament but conducted very publicly through the press and on television. The very fact that both Parliament and the public believed that numbers from the Commonwealth had to be limited, indicated that there was something wrong about immigration and that the nation needed to be protected from these newcomers. This was incredibly hurtful to communities such as those from Jamaica with their very pro-British culture and migrants who came here expecting a warm welcome.

The openly racist speech of Enoch Powell MP which was delivered to a Conservative Association meeting, in Birmingham on April 20, 1968, was an enormous blow to immigrants who were actively seeking integration and to contribute positively to the society where they had chosen to live. Mr Powell not only opposed further immigration and advocated repatriation of many of those already here, but he opposed the introduction of laws forbidding discrimination. He said:

> "As Mr Heath has put it, we will have no first-class citizens and second-class citizens. This does not mean that the immigrant and his descendants should be elevated into a privileged or special class or that the citizen should be denied his right to discriminate in the management of his own affairs between one fellow-citizen and another or that he should be subjected to imposition as to his reasons and motive for behaving in one lawful manner rather than another."[10]

2.11 Powellism

Enoch Powell was dismissed from the Shadow Cabinet by Edward Heath, following this speech which virtually marked the end of his political career. But his support in the country came from unexpected sources. A march in the East End of London by dockers and meat porters in support of a right wing Tory MP — a traditional enemy of the working classes — was a great surprise to many. For those familiar with the sociological concept of 'relative deprivation' it was a gift.

The experience of deprivation drives together those who fear the loss of their few remaining privileges in society.

It was not the middle class professionals or the Members of Parliament who were losing out through immigration. They were well protected in the areas where they lived, and by their academic and professional qualifications, but the working classes were in daily competition for jobs and houses and sexual partners (possible spouses). Their one high status was that they were 'white', in a predominantly white society in which the traditional mores put the black man in a lower category of social differentiation. This was now threatened by the Race Relations Bill of 1968 which would remove the right of discrimination that Enoch Powell had maintained was a fundamental human right enshrined in British social history.

2.12 Race Relations

The Act was passed, and became the most significant piece of legislation in its field in Britain. It was the culmination of a series of Acts, beginning with the Commonwealth Immigrants Act 1962, which was strengthened in 1968, and the Race Relations Act of 1965. The 1968 Race Relations Act showed the clear determination of the British Government to establish complete equality of treatment for all people, regardless of race, colour or creed, in every sphere of human relationships in which legislation can regulate.

Nevertheless, by 1968 the die was already cast in the eyes of many immigrants from the West Indies and other parts of the Commonwealth who knew that their hopes of full integration would not be achieved in their lifetime. The areas of immigrant settlement were all places where a multitude of social problems already existed and their presence tended to exacerbate these — at least, that was the perception of those who lived there.

Despite Edward Heath's declaration that there would be no second-class citizens, Stuart Hall had already foreseen the significance of what was happening in these inner-city areas. He wrote:

> The problems of the young immigrants are the problems of marginal men and women of British society — Britain's new second-class citizens. Few people have begun to understand the stresses placed on them or their complex needs and expectations or their particular vulnerability. Before we try to find solutions to their 'problems', we must imagine ourselves in their place. We must try to understand what it is like for them, standing at the point of conflict and intersection between two worlds — one world, which carries echoes, associations, memories and ideals of the past and another which carries the promise — but also the threat and the danger — of the future.[11]

That threat and danger were never understood by our political leaders. In those days Commonwealth immigrants had no representation in Parliament. Middle class MPs had no personal experience of living and working in areas of migrant settlement, and working class MPs, even if they still lived in areas where migrants had settled, were all too aware of the fears and prejudices of their traditional voters. The result was that the few lone voices calling attention to the serious social and cultural issues that were already embedded in the inner-city areas of our major cities were either sidelined or ignored. My own books,[12] drawing attention to these issues, received brief national coverage in the press, radio and television, but were soon forgotten. They were made the subject of television socio-documentaries, but these were mostly regarded by the media for their entertainment value rather than alerting the nation to issues that, if not addressed, would one day result in the Tottenham riots of August 2011.

Notes

[1] 'Black' as a term referring to African and African-Caribbeans was never used in those days. In fact many of the fair-skinned newcomers who enjoyed high status in the West Indies' colour code of social class would have felt insulted if they had been addressed as 'black'. The polite term was 'coloured' or 'non-white'.

[2] I was at that time in happy ignorance of the fact that black Pentecostals do not approve of dancing!

[3] Clifford Hill, *Black and White in Harmony*, Hodder and Stoughton, London, 1958, p. 24.

[4] *Ibid.*, p. 28.

[5] Rocksteady music with a strong beat was popular in Jamaica in the early 1960s and it later developed into Reggae around 1968.

[6] Stuart Hall, *The Young Englanders*, National Committee for Commonwealth Immigrants, London, 1967.

[7] Clifford Hill, *Black and White in Harmony*, Hodder and Stoughton, London, 1958, p. 43.

[8] *op. cit.*, p. 9.

[9] *Ibid.*, p. 10.

[10] *The Times*, 21 April 1968.

[11] See *op. cit.*, p. 14.

[12] Clifford Hill, *West Indian Migrants and the London Churches*, Oxford;, 1963; *How Colour Prejudiced is Britain?* Gollancz; *Race: A Christian Symposium*, Gollancz, 1968; *Immigration and Integration*, Pergamon, 1969.

Chapter Three

LIFE IN THE CARIBBEAN IN 1962

3.1 Visiting the West Indies

In 1962 I went to the West Indies as an envoy of the British Council of Churches, visiting Barbados, Trinidad and Jamaica. The purpose of the visit was in part fact-finding and, in part, relationship-building. The particular concern in Britain was that large numbers of immigrants were coming from the islands where they had strong links with churches of all the mainline denominations, but once they reached cities in England they lost all contact with the church. Most of the churches with which I was familiar in London had no contact at all with churches in the West Indian islands, and my job was to explore the possibility of creating these links. My tour was well-planned and I was not only welcomed by churches, but in Jamaica the Government provided a social worker to take me on a tour of the island to see community projects and schools as well as meeting with church leaders and community workers.

One of the things that surprised me when I arrived in Barbados was how very British everything was. Bridgetown, Barbados was my first port of call where the name of Admiral Lord Nelson was honoured, despite his well-documented derogatory views of black Africans. In travelling around the island it seemed that every village had an English name.

However, it was not only the names of towns and streets that were British, but also the major social institutions of government and education. This was less noticeable in Trinidad, where the Spanish colonial influence was still strong, but it was particularly noticeable in Jamaica after three hundred years of British rule. In schools I was surprised to discover that the teaching of history was all about the kings and queens of England and very little on their own social history.

3.2 Slavery Taboo

There was another thing that surprised me— no one wanted to talk about slavery. It was almost a taboo subject that was not even spoken about within the family. It was in the past. That was the view taken by most people: that was where it should stay —in the past, not a subject for today. They did not want to speak about it. In some of the rural areas I visited in Jamaica there were the ruins of former sugar estates, with decaying 'great houses' and slave quarters, but local residents were quite unwilling to talk about the past and were often embarrassed in responding to my questions. It was made clear to me that slavery was not an acceptable subject for discussion.

The exception was in the shanty towns of West Kingston where the ganja-smoking Ras Tafarians reigned supreme. They were a constant thorn in the side of the Jamaican Government as they had no desire to play any part in the life of the nation. Some were said to be descendants of the Maroons, the fierce communities of rebels established by escaped slaves who had occupied inaccessible places in the Blue Mountains and evaded all endeavours of capture by the British colonial rulers of the island. The Rastas regarded Africa as their true home and Haile Selassie as the Messiah who would one day come to release them from the bondage of 'Babylon' and take them back to their true home in Africa, to freedom from the white man's world of oppression.

3.3 Fears of Violence

My hosts in Jamaica insisted on providing a police escort for these visits. I foolishly said this was not necessary and boasted about my work in London, saying that I had been in many areas of conflict involving people from the Caribbean and I had never been harmed. But when I was surrounded by hostile crowds among the shanties I was only too pleased to stay close to my burly police sergeant and to allow him to lead the way. In fact, before I got out of the car, a bearded head complete with dreadlocks thrust through the open window, saying, "Independence! White man!" He then drew his finger across his neck while making a bloodcurdling sound. It was somewhat unnerving, very different from my privileged position among the migrants in London!

My visit was shortly before Jamaica's independence from Britain, and there were many rumours that it would be a time of great bloodshed accompanied by a political revolution led by the dispossessed, overturning the power structures of the elite who were the fair-skinned legacy of the white 'plantocracy' who had ruled Jamaica throughout the three hundred years of colonial domination.

Living conditions in the shanty towns were appalling, and in the early 1960s poverty and unemployment were rife. The Government tried repeatedly to destroy these slum areas and to discourage people from moving in to them from the rural villages in search of work that just was not available. Each area was run by a local warlord who was surrounded by his henchmen. He was also a drugs baron and exercised control over all his residents while fiercely defending his turf.

3.4 The Slave Trade

Having researched the eighteenth century slave trade and the fifty year struggle for the abolition of slavery in the British Empire, I expected to encounter hostility and demands for reparation. Instead, with the exception of the leaders of the West Kingston slum dwellers, everywhere I went I was surrounded by great goodwill, generosity and expressions of affection for Britain. I found this almost embarrassing because I was aware of the history of the Caribbean islands and the notorious Atlantic slave trade triangle, in which Britain had played a large part, transporting manufactured goods from Liverpool and Bristol to the West Coast of Africa. There the ships were transformed into slavers with carpenters working to install the shelves where the Africans would be chained for the voyage across the Atlantic to the Americas and the Caribbean islands, a voyage that could take up to three months at sea. Finally, on the third leg of the triangle, sugar, rum and tobacco would be transported back to Britain. It was a lucrative trade and large numbers of the population in England bought shares in the ships and benefited from their profits.

I was very much aware that the wealth of Britain in the eighteenth century, which paved the way for the future prosperity of the nineteenth century Victorian era, had largely come from slavery. The Industrial Revolution that blossomed during the second half of the eighteenth century was greatly aided by the Merchant Navy opening up overseas markets. Manufacturing could not have developed so rapidly without these markets. Goods produced in the factories of the Midlands and in the cotton mills of Lancashire and the woollen mills of Yorkshire were sold overseas, while in Britain and the rest of Europe there was an increasing demand for sugar, that could not be satisfied from home-grown sugar beet. Thus the plantations in the Caribbean became hugely important, and it was thought that the demand for labour at that time could only be satisfied by the importation of increasing numbers of enslaved Africans.

In the year 1800, some 75% of the British economy was in some way linked with the slave trade and colonial slavery. This was the reason why Wilberforce and his parliamentary colleagues met with such fierce opposition every time they attempted to introduce a Bill to limit or abolish the slave trade. I was very aware of the monumental injustice of the slave trade and of the cruelty of plantation slavery, so the level of goodwill I encountered was a great surprise. The pro-British sentiment was particularly strong in Barbados and Jamaica. In Barbados, I was reminded that the island had been the first colony in the British Empire to declare war against Germany in 1939 in support of Britain. They were proud of their 'Britishness' and the fact that their soldiers had fought alongside British and Commonwealth forces in the Second World War.

3.5 'Going Home'

In Jamaica, it was not only in the towns, but also in the rural areas that there was open goodwill expressed towards Britain. Would-be emigrants spoke of their eagerness to 'go home' although they had never been to Britain. This was no doubt inherited from the white colonials who spoke of returning to Britain with such enthusiasm that it set a social pattern. They evidently painted a picture of their homeland in such glowing terms that travelling to Britain became established in the minds of the masses as the most desirable ambition. It was a country where everything was perfect. And of course it was the land from which the missionaries had come who had brought the Christian faith to the islands, and therefore it was seen as a Christian country upholding all the finest ideals and biblical values of society.

England was seen as the natural home of the Jamaican people, and they were confident that they would be received with the same warmth as they felt for British people. In listening to them I couldn't help feeling guilty, knowing the attitude I had left behind in London, and knowing the bitter experience, the disappointment and disillusionment of many of the eager young people who had taken the great leap of faith and travelled to Britain. I knew what awaited many of these young hopefuls, and while I urged caution, and spoke of some of the difficulties faced by immigrants, I did not feel at liberty to indulge in too much detail which might spoil the main purpose of my visit — to establish good working relationships between churches in the West Indies and churches in areas of immigrant settlement in Britain.

3.6 Family and Marriage

From the many conversations I had with people both in the farming communities and in the towns, I learned a great deal about the social structure and family life of people in Jamaica, where I spent most of my time. My social worker escort was very open in talking to me about the customs in the different communities I visited. In one rural community there were preparations for a wedding and I talked to both the bride and groom, who were both aged about 55 and were grandparents. It was explained to me that this was the social custom. It clearly derived from the period of colonial slavery when marriage was forbidden to slaves under colonial law.

Many slaves did go through an unofficial form of 'marriage' in their community after the spread of Christianity, due to the work of the missionaries. But slaves were always liable to be sold to another plantation and couples could not guarantee being kept in permanent residential situations. Marriage, nevertheless, was seen to be highly desirable, in the style of the daughter of a plantation owner, who lived in the great house. When she married, there would be a great celebration. All the 'county' folk would come for the wedding reception following a church ceremony, and the slaves would all be allowed to join in celebrations in some form. This set the pattern of marriage: a church service, followed by a great reception to which family members and the local community would be invited but also people from other villages would come to join in the festivities — they didn't need invitations! All this, of course, would cost money, and this was the major reason why people in poor communities delayed their marriage until they could afford to marry in the style they had inherited from colonial days, and to pay for a feast for a large number of people.

Marriage thus became associated with a particular stratum in society, and the custom in the rural communities was that of 'faithful concubinage' or 'common law marriage' — a socially acceptable form of cohabitation. Often, in the past, couples would have engaged in a form of commitment within their community whereby they were recognised as a cohabiting couple. But marriage was for those who could afford it, and the children and grandchildren would all take part in the church ceremony and reception. The large number from surrounding villages at the reception included many who had not been invited, but they were never turned away.

3.7 Common-Law Unions and the Role of Women

I remember discussing the subject of marriage with one younger couple who had several children. I asked him why he did not marry as he appeared more affluent than many other couples. He humorously replied (at least I think it was meant to be humorous!), "I marry: I buy her shoes. I don't marry: she buy her own shoes." I addressed the same question to his common law spouse and she replied, "I marry: he beat me, I can't leave him. I don't marry: he beat me, I leave him." I did not pursue the subject, recognising that I was out of my cultural comfort zone!

My visit to the West Indies was shortly after the publication of two seminal studies of family life in the West Indies, from which I had learned a great deal in advance of my visit. These two studies, which are still today regarded as classics, were *My Mother Who Fathered Me*,[1] by Edith Clarke, and *Family and Culture in Jamaica*,[2] by Fernando Henriques. I was keen to do my own research and check some of the conclusions reached in these two studies, particularly in relation to the legacy of slavery.

My social worker companion was particularly helpful throughout my visits, especially in remote rural areas where the local accent or 'patois' was not always easy for me to understand. She was also a mine of information on local customs and social history. She took me to see the ruins of a colonial house and what remained of the slave quarters, and the place on the estate where the sugar production plant would have been. It was a nostalgic experience that helped me to understand the numerous books I had read on that period and the research I had done on the records presented to Parliament by the abolitionists.

I saw for myself the small, overcrowded houses in which some families lived on tiny smallholdings that could only have provided them with a bare subsistence level of income. These smallholdings were themselves a legacy of slavery, and were part of the movement onto vacant land in the aftermath of the emancipation of 1838. This common land was usually of poorer quality or more inaccessible than that of the larger estates owned by the colonial planters.

Many of these small farms were owned by women, and it was quite usual for inheritance to pass down through the female line. The women were the stable units in the community, providing for their children often without the support of a man. This, too, was a legacy of slavery — from the practice on the sugar estates for the older women, who were not strong enough to work in the field gangs, to spend their days caring for the children. From this there developed the important role of the 'grannies' in Jamaican society. In rural and working class communities most children in the 1960s were brought up by their grannies who acted as head of the family, teaching acceptable behavioural standards and asserting strict discipline.

3.8 Sex and Pregnancy

In the rural communities that I visited it was not uncommon for adolescent children to engage in sex experimentation with different partners, and a girl would continue such behaviour until she became pregnant. When this happened there was a kind of ritual —a kind of community charade which was played out. Her mother would fly into a great rage, shouting and abusing the girl and driving her out of the household, saying that she had brought disgrace upon the family. The girl would then seek refuge in the home of an aunt or some other relative in a neighbouring village where she would stay maybe for a few days, or for a few weeks, after which the relative would go to visit the girl's mother and make representations on behalf of the girl until reconciliation was effected. After this it was usual for the mother to take her daughter back into her house until the baby was born, when she would then care for the baby as her own child.

This allowed the girl to resume her normal life, completing her schooling or other training, and she would be available for a long-term relationship with either the father of her child or another man. The fact that she already had a child would be considered to demonstrate her fecundity and suitability as a wife and mother. In most rural and working class communities a girl would be allowed one 'fall from grace', but if she had a second or third pregnancy before settling with a partner she would be considered 'a loose woman'. Once she acquired an unsavoury reputation she would be considered unsuitable for a long-term or permanent partnership.

For men, the situation was very different. A whole different set of social mores seemed to apply to boys and young men. They were expected to desire to sow their wild oats and to distribute their favours among a number of girls. In rural communities it would be unusual for a young man to settle down in a long-term domiciliary relationship with a girl while still in his youth. Working class rural Jamaican matriarchal society made no such demands upon young men. Youthful marriage was out of the question. That would come later, following a period of common law union, which in Jamaican society of the 1960s was the norm in most rural communities. It would be in later life, when the couple were grandparents, and had achieved a certain level of prosperity, that they would mark their improved social status by marriage in the customary manner with a church service and a feast provided for the whole community.

3.9 Marriage

Marriage was just another social custom that in 1960s Jamaica still bore the marks of slavery. Social class in the Caribbean was also heavily influenced by colonial slavery. The colour code that is endemic to class in West Indian society also had its origins in colonial slavery, and is still today part of the surviving legacy of that heinous institution. The white men regularly used the African slaves for their own sexual gratification. The brutality of these sexual relationships began on the slave ships and subsequently became an institutionalised practice on the plantations. These practices are well-documented in numerous studies of that period and they were often brought to the attention of the nation through research carried out by members of the Clapham Group who supplied William Wilberforce with factual information for his abolitionist speeches in Parliament.

When Parliament and the humanitarians, notably the Nonconformist Churches, began to scrutinise West Indian slavery in the late 18th century, they were appalled by the tales of sexual laxity and licence — slave women unable to resist the advances of their masters; slaves casually offered to visiting friends; beatings and punishments when sexual advances were spurned. All these stories, common throughout the Caribbean, were unexceptional; part of the very fabric of slave society and quite distinct from the more outrageous and sadistic acts of sexual violation. Tales spread in London of slaves sleeping with masters to avoid beatings; of reluctant women being flogged to within an inch of their lives.... When whites visited friends on neighbouring estates on Sundays, or following an evening drinking, it was common to have women selected upon the properties for the purpose of sleeping with these visitors.[3]

3.10 Colour Code and Social Class

This sexual activity inevitably produced children of a lighter colour, who were not forced to work in the field gangs or in the gangs that worked in the sugar mills. They were given privileged positions in the households of the plantocracy. This produced a hierarchy in which the lighter-skinned individuals became the elites in slave society. Those who were indistinguishable from whites were usually set free and became part of a new elitist group of mixed race. It was also common practice for slave owners to bequeath, on their death, freedom to favourite slaves who had served them faithfully. The free men and women, usually of lighter skin colour, formed a privileged class in colonial days, which carried over and developed following emancipation.

This colour code of social class was still very evident in the 1960s, and those who were of the darkest skin were often the most socially deprived. It was usually the ambition of darker-skinned people to marry someone of lighter skin and to produce children of lighter skin, especially if they became more economically prosperous. The absence of the recognition of this colour code in relationships between immigrants and the host community in Britain was one of the sore points in the experience of many lighter-skinned migrants. The British didn't recognise any differentiation and simply treated everyone as 'coloured'.

3.11 Social and Cultural Norms

All the major social institutions in Jamaica in the 1960s reflected those of Britain, which would no doubt have gone back to the days of colonial slavery and then have become institutionalised in the colonial Government. The structure of democratic parliamentary government was modelled on that of the Westminster Parliament, with the franchise extended to all its citizens. The systems of law enforcement, police services and court procedures were all similar to those in Britain. Education, from primary school to university, was also modelled upon the British education system. The thing that I found surprising was that even the English examination system, and the teaching of many subjects, also followed the British model. I had expected some similarities, but with the addition of local Caribbean history. This appeared to be missing from the curriculum in schools I visited.

I visited churches of most denominations, finding great similarities, although inevitably differences in the style of music, and greater freedom of worship and participation in some of the congregations. Churches of all the mainline denominations found in Britain were present and had large followings. In addition, there were churches founded by

American missionaries, often drawing support and resources from an American base. These were usually Pentecostal in origins and theological doctrines. The overall impression was that the Christian churches were strongly linked to Western roots and largely followed the teaching and practices of the denominations with which they were associated.

There were, of course, many cultural differences which were unique to the Caribbean peoples, with each of the islands having distinctive features. These cultural differences reflected African origins which were more to be seen in rural areas, often reflecting what I regarded as superstitious elements, such as fears of the darkness. Small farming families taking their goods to a market town would often have a long walk carrying heavy loads. They would set off during the night, but going in small parties, singing hymns along the way. I originally thought that this was an expression of religious faith and an indication of the way in which Christianity was practised in the island, but I was told that it was to keep the 'duppies' at bay – to drive away the evil spirits who might assail them on their journey.

Funerals were also different, and after a death the playing of drums and singing would go on throughout the night. At the service around the grave, as I had already noticed in England, the family and close friends insisted upon doing the filling of the grave themselves. This usually took a very long time, and was accompanied throughout by the singing of hymns (which, in England, undertakers often found difficult to fit in with their tight schedules).

3.12 Generosity

My overall impression of the Jamaican people was highly favourable. Of course, life proceeded at a slower pace than I was used to in England. In many ways this was a welcome break from being driven by tight timetables back home. Returning to England by banana boat — where the bananas were the first class passengers (they were the ones with air-conditioned cabins!) — was slow, but it gave me a little space to reflect and write my notes before plunging back into the whirlpool of London.

I had suffered somewhat from the heat as the homes where I stayed did not have air conditioning, and many of them lacked the kind of comforts to which I was used. But everywhere I went, even in the poorest communities, I was greeted with great openness and generous hospitality. Having survived the brutal experience of three centuries of oppression at the hands of the British, they were still prepared to welcome me from the nation that had treated them so cruelly. I found this a completely humbling experience. My love for the Jamaican people, and my admiration for them, increased enormously. I was left in no doubt that the Jamaican people loved the British, but I returned to London wondering how much of the bitter experience of the migrants in Britain would be relayed home and change attitudes in the future.

Notes

[1] Edith Clarke, *My Mother who Fathered Me, a Study of The Families in Three Selected Communities of Jamaica*, The Press, University of the West Indies, Kingston, Jamaica, 1999 (First edition, 1957).

[2] Fernando Henriques, *Family and Culture in Jamaica*, Eyre and Spottiswoode, London, 1953.

[3] James Walvin, *Black Ivory – Slavery in the British Empire*, Blackwell Publishing, London, 2004, p. 190.

Chapter Four

TOTTENHAM IN THE 1960s

4.1 Life in Tottenham

I was married by the time I left Harlesden, moving to Tottenham where we spent most of the 1960s. Many of the same social issues that we had become used to in west London were there in north London. Immigration from the Caribbean and from West Africa had already made an impact, and in many streets white residents were moving out, which was changing the complexion of the neighbourhood as more immigrants moved in. We were both very active in the community and it was during this time that we saw the beginnings of the social revolution which has engulfed the area and brought about the fundamental changes that have given rise to the present situation. But what was it like in the 1960s – fifty years ago? Here is an extract from my notebook:

March 1961

"I'm dying, Parson. I'll be dead in an hour. I want you to say a prayer for me before I die." A big, heavily built brown-skinned man of Caribbean origin lurched along Tottenham High Road, coming towards me with long, slow swaying strides. It looked as though he was optimistic in giving himself an hour. Each step looked as though it could be his last. I half expected him to pitch forward onto his face at any moment. To forestall this I stepped forward and took his arm, steering him through the church car park into the hall. He sank heavily into the nearest chair, his head bowed, a picture of dejection. Tears welled in his eyes and rolled down his cheeks reaching the lapel of his jacket.

"What makes you think you're going to die?" I asked.

"I've taken fifty aspirins," was the laconic reply. "Say a prayer for me, Parson. I had to do it. There's no other way. I can't get anywhere to live. Nobody wants a family with three kids. There's a note in my pocket for my wife. Tell her, I'm sorry. There's no other way."

The tears which had slowed up during the speech now increased to a steady stream. He bowed his head in his hands, elbows on his knees, massive shoulders shaking with emotion – a picture of helpless despair.

I knew something of the story behind this man's present predicament. It was less than four years since I had married him to a pretty little Jamaican girl with dancing eyes and dimpled cheeks. Whenever I called to see her she had to come down three flights of stairs from the one attic room, where she and her husband lived with their twins and a third child, for which they paid rent of nearly four pounds a week – a fortune in those days.

She was no longer the laughing carefree girl I remembered from when they had first come to see me to book their marriage. Like her husband she was desperately anxious to find somewhere else to live. For some months they had lived under the shadow of a notice of dismissal which their landlord had served upon them following a difference of views and a heated exchange of words upon some trivial subject. When they had failed to get out on the due date the landlord had taken them to court where they had been given three months to vacate their room.

Throughout the weeks since the court hearing, both husband and wife had tramped the streets inquiring for a room to let. They had scanned the accommodation columns of the local newspaper, made enquiries among their friends, studied the advertisement cards in the windows of newspaper shops, many of which said "No Coloured" or "Sorry: no Coloured, no Irish and no dogs". All their inquiries were to no avail.

All this went through my mind as I looked at the dejected figure in front of me. I had had sufficient experience of suicides and attempted suicide to know that his life was in no immediate danger, but there were certain practical concerns that were urgent.

"How many aspirins were in the bottle?" I asked.

"One hundred," he responded.

"Where's the bottle now?" I demanded.

"I dropped it behind the seat in the park," he said.

"For the next child to come along and pick up and swallow," I said, pointedly.

"I don't want to hurt anyone," he whined, "I just want to die."

"Come on, get up man," I said with a roughness that belied the sympathy I was feeling for him. "We've got to find those aspirins before they get into a child's hands." He pulled himself drunkenly to his feet and swayed unsteadily beside me as we walked through the church car park and across the High Road into the tiny park in front of the Town Hall. A half-empty bottle of aspirins lay on the ground behind the bench to which he pointed. Beside it lay an empty Coke bottle that he had used to swill down the tablets.

He refused to go with me to the hospital so I persuaded him to walk back with me to the church hall and sit under the surveillance of a young man on the staff of our youth club. I left him for a while, returning shortly after, hoping to find him sufficiently drowsy to move him to hospital without much trouble. I was disappointed to find him impatiently demanding the return of the bottle so that he could finish the job speedily.

Four or five young men from my youth group stood by while I tried, ineffectively, to persuade him to walk with me to the Prince of Wales Hospital next door. Finally, I sent one of the young men to telephone for an ambulance. The two medics were as unsuccessful as I had been. Nothing would budge him. He just wanted to be left alone, to stay there until he died. The ambulance driver radioed for the police. A squad car and three policemen were soon on the spot. They held a council of war in the car park with the two ambulance men. "You can't force a man to go to hospital" said the driver.

"It's simple," said a short, thickset uniformed constable, rubbing his hands together, "We'll arrest him!"

"You can't do that!" I exploded. "He hasn't done anything criminal."

"Now this is what we'll do," said a massive sergeant with the quiet air of the authority of one who had seen it all before. "You want to get rid of him, right? Well, we'll come in and eject him. Once he's outside, the ambulance men try to persuade him to get into the ambulance. He puts up a struggle and we knock him off for a breach of the peace." He thrust his hands on his hips with an air of evident satisfaction that defied anyone to oppose him.

"I'll have one more try," I said, turning my back on them and striding back into the church hall. "Listen man, the police are here now," I said, taking the would-be suicide firmly by the arm. "You don't want any trouble from them, do you? Now get up and come with me." We all held our breath as he slowly pulled himself to his feet and allowed me to lead him outside and straight into the ambulance. Two of the policeman and one medic jumped in beside him. The doors were closed and the ambulance drove away to the local General Hospital.

Later in the evening, my wife called to see his wife. It was as well she did, for no one had bothered to notify her of her husband's trouble. As far as she knew he had simply gone out to look for accommodation. The next day, when he still failed to come home and there was no news of him from either the hospital or the police, she took the three children with her and walked to the General Hospital in St Ann's Road. There she was told that her husband had refused treatment and had been 'sectioned' and sent to a secure psychiatric institution in another part of London.

4.2 Cold Comfort

This was just one more incident that went into my notebook of the way black people were treated in this country in the early 1960s. No white person would have received similar treatment because their relatives would have gone straight to their MP and got their story into the press. In fact, it did not occur to the hospital authorities that a West Indian girl would be just as worried about the unaccountable absence of her husband as an English wife.

"They don't feel the same as we do", I heard an English social worker, with many years' experience, declare to a large gathering of professionals who were considering the problems of working among black immigrants. "They have so many kids," she said, "and they live in such appalling conditions they don't even know who the kids belong to half the time. They're just looked after by anyone in the house."

It was attitudes like this among professional people that caused deep resentment among those who had left their homes in the Caribbean Islands with a profound love for Britain and the expectation that there would be work for them and a warm welcome in the 'Mother Country'. Instead, when they came as immigrants, they were treated with cold disdain by the middle and professional classes, and with resentment by the working classes with whom they were in daily contact and often in competition for work and housing.

Even when they went to church the immigrants were not guaranteed a welcome. Their natural warmth and friendliness were often not matched, and they sat alone on a hard pew in a half empty church. No one came and sat with them or spoke to them after the service. Of course, English people don't normally go and sit beside strangers in public places, even in church, but the newcomers were not familiar with this peculiarly British culture. If there was one place they really expected to be made welcome it was in church. There was usually no open hostility, but they interpreted the English cold formality as a sign that they were not welcome.

4.3 Churches and Immigrants

There were, however, some churches where the clergy were afraid of losing their regular congregation if too many black faces were seen entering the church. I heard lots of stories of immigrants not feeling welcome in various churches, but I only had one first-hand experience of this. St Philip's, in Philip Lane, Tottenham, drew most of its congregation from the dwindling remnant of middle class residents in the area. On one occasion in the early 1960s when a West Indian ventured into the Sunday morning service he was politely told that he should go to the church where I was the minister, on Tottenham High Road. The following Sunday the man recounted his experience to me. I immediately sought a meeting with the vicar and he admitted that it was true. He justified his action by saying that he genuinely thought the man would feel more comfortable in my congregation where there were many other Caribbeans, rather than in his all-white congregation.

Even in my own church, where we had hundreds of black people attending, there were tensions. One couple who had attended the church for many years and had relocated to Enfield, an upmarket middle class area in those days, more in keeping with her status as a local magistrate, found their usual pew occupied by a black family when she and her husband came one Sunday to evening worship just as the service started. They turned around and left the church and never came again. But they were unusual, even among those who had moved out of the area to live in the more salubrious suburbs north of Tottenham. Most of the white congregation accepted the newcomers as part of the changing patterns of daily life in the area.

Most of those who had moved away remained loyal to the church where they had grown up and continued to commute regularly on Sundays and to be an active part of the community. Although the church treasurer told me when I arrived on the scene in the late 1950s that my objective should be to bring in some 'good middle class people' to strengthen the church, most of the congregation recognised that in a situation of rapid demographic change the church had to respond to the local situation and meet the needs of the neighbourhood if it was to survive.

My reputation had gone ahead of me when we moved from west London, and my church at High Cross on Tottenham High Road soon began to attract large numbers of Africans and Caribbeans. We ensured that a warm welcome awaited them and we made every effort to include them in our regular activities with special provision for their particular needs. We had a Nigerian Christian Fellowship that regularly met in our home, and several Caribbean associations which allowed people from different islands to meet with one another in a safe and convivial environment.

4.4 Media Exposure

I had kept a considerable body of notes throughout my ministry in west London and shortly after arriving in Tottenham I published my first book, *Black and White in Harmony*. This brought invitations to serve on local and national committees. I also took part in — or acted as adviser to — numerous BBC radio and television and Independent Television programmes, which inevitably increased the profile of High Cross Church and attracted both welcome and unwelcome attention! The latter came from the National Front, who for some weeks in 1961 picketed members of my congregation on their way into the church on Tottenham High Road.

The BBC commissioned me to do a series of weekly broadcasts on the BBC Caribbean Service. Each week I used to go to Bush House in central London to record an update on life in the immigrant communities in London, giving news and comment about living conditions and community events. On one occasion in May 1961 our morning service was broadcast by the BBC from High Cross Church. Word of mouth went round that it was not only to be broadcast in Britain but also in the Caribbean. It was Commonwealth Sunday and it attracted a larger than usual number of West Indian immigrants. The church, which seated 1,000, was full, so the service was relayed into the church hall that seated 500, which was also full. Several hundred more were standing in the car park listening to the service on loudspeakers. It was the largest congregation the Tottenham church had ever seen.

4.5 House Attacked

During the sermon in a throwaway remark, I said something to the effect that I would rather my daughter married a committed Christian from the black community than an unbelieving white boy. The effect was explosive – not with my congregation who were familiar with my views – but abusive letters by the sack load poured in from all parts of the country. My daughter was only three at the time so my remark was somewhat academic, but it was picked up in the national press, and several papers carried a picture of my daughter and myself, which was not helpful to the cause of good community relationships, as my statement was taken out of context. But the very idea of a white girl marrying a black man in 1961 Britain was presented as sensational news!

Two weeks later, on a Saturday night in June 1961, extremists from the National Front attacked my house in Downhills Park Road, Tottenham. My family and I were actually away on holiday at the time. Neighbours said they heard a car draw up outside the house, which led to the speculation that they came from outside the borough. The attackers threw white paint over the front door and windows. They also painted insulting slogans on the wooden fence at the side of the house — **RACE MIXING PRIEST**. On the pavement in front of the house they painted in huge letters the words — **NIGGER LOVER**.[1] Also on the pavement they left the letters 'BNP'. Those who painted these words, of course, meant them to be insulting. But in a strange kind of way this attack, although quite frightening for my family at the time, probably represented the highest accolade I had been accorded.

The words remained there throughout Sunday and were seen by the neighbours and many passers-by. Someone evidently informed the press, and photographers came taking pictures of the house and the pavement. The police were informed and they began an investigation but we were never told about the result. On Monday morning there was a swift reaction from the Local Authority. The Tottenham Council sent workmen to obliterate the offending words, but they were accompanied by press photographers who were keen to see what would be done.

The words were obliterated on the wooden fence but the pavement presented a particular problem. The Council workmen were unable to get rid of the words on the paving slabs so they simply turned the stones over. As far as I am aware that 'hate message' is still there in front of my former home in Downhills Park Road, Tottenham, but hidden from public view. It is a little parable of the way racism remains in our national life in Britain – hidden from sight by a veneer of respectability, and controlled by legislation enforcing 'political correctness'.

Legislation can control behaviour, but it cannot change attitudes. They only respond to the slow pressures of cultural change which sometimes take more than a generation to effect. The incident represented the institutionalised racism which is just one element in a complex amalgam of social tensions that eventually exploded in the Broadwater Farm disturbances on 6 October 1985, and onto Tottenham High Street on 6 August 2011 — almost exactly fifty years after my house was attacked.

At that time I wrote about the issues and the future danger, I spoke at numerous public meetings, I spoke on national radio and appeared on many television programmes, warning of the dangers that lay ahead unless the issues of the day were addressed, but no one was listening. No-one was interested in helping the newcomers to settle and integrate into society in this country. The only subject that was given much attention was how to control the numbers of immigrants coming in to Britain. That was the big political debate in 1961.

4.6 Reaction to Attack

The reaction of my own church leaders to this attack on the church house and the picketing of our congregation was interesting. They immediately called a meeting, but they did not invite me! I learned of their intention by chance and I immediately left my family on holiday in Yorkshire and travelled back to Tottenham. I walked into the meeting and took the chair as I would normally have done. I turned it into a prayer meeting, asking God what we should do under these circumstances when the ministry of the church was under attack. The result was quite remarkable in the ensuing discussion. Instead of the church leaders voting to dismiss me as I suspected, there was a closing of ranks in the face of opposition, and a determination to continue our policy of being open to people of all races, and to meeting the needs of the different sections of the local population. It was a milestone in the work of the High Cross Church. Our numbers of both white and 'coloured' worshippers continued to increase. The church, which was widely reported to have the largest congregation of ethnic immigrants in Britain, attracted a lot of media attention. It was often full which, when most church congregations were declining in the 1960s, was against the trends.[2]

Support from the local community was very encouraging. Our youth work flourished and so did our outreach in many other ways. We aimed to discover where there were gaps in meeting the needs in our catchment area, one of which was working with people with disabilities and those who were housebound. We had a regular weeknight meeting for them, and we mobilised a fleet of cars from members of the congregation who provided transport for them.

In meeting the needs of the different ethnic communities our flourishing Nigerian Fellowship catered mainly for students living in our area. They were not the only group to meet in our home. So too did our youth group most Sunday nights. It was not easy coping with all the pressures of these meetings and the hospitality responsibilities which fell heavily upon my wife, who by this time also had two young children to care for. Somehow we managed, and our children thrived. We also had a variety of church-based meetings and activities for the West Indian community, who were very much larger than the African. Our West Indian quartet of singers became nationally known after we had used them in broadcasts from the church.

The Borough Council was very supportive of our work and during the time we were in Tottenham I became Mayor's Chaplain three times — twice in Tottenham and once in Haringey after the reorganisation of London boroughs. A number of Members of the local Council were also keen members of High Cross Church and active in a lot of our programmes. I was involved in many local community organisations, as well as being a member of the

National Committee for Commonwealth Immigrants and being consulted by the Home Office on issues relating to Commonwealth immigration and the settlement of migrants, although I cannot claim any success in influencing national policy. The politicians had their own agendas.

4.7 Relationships with Other Churches

My biggest disappointment was that churches in other areas of London seemed uninterested in reaching out to meet the needs of those settling in their areas. I felt that an enormous opportunity was being lost. Through the Institute of Race Relations I directed a piece of research across churches of all the major denominations in the Greater London area. The results were published by Oxford University Press in book form in 1963.[3] The survey showed that only 4% of the West Indian migrant population were in attendance at the six major branches of the Christian church in London – the Roman Catholic, the Church of England, the Baptist, Congregational, Methodist and Presbyterian churches. This compared with an average of 69% of the total population in the British Caribbean islands who regularly attended one or other of same churches. These figures did not include numbers for Pentecostals or other smaller Christian groups, which were not available at that time.

The fact of such a massive falling away in church attendance by the Caribbean migrants was undoubtedly an indictment of church leaders of all denominations. My own experience was that it was not difficult to attract the migrants to come to church. They were only too eager to attend where a warm welcome awaited them. The fact that they boycotted the English churches and began to establish their own was a source of considerable grief to me, and I wrote and spoke about it extensively.

In a paper that I read to a conference of sociologists at

Senate House in the University of London in January 1969, I gave some reasons why West Indians were rejecting churchgoing in Britain:

> The West Indian comes from a predominantly English cultural background in which most of his major social institutions are based upon the English ideal types. Probably the most outstanding example of this is religion, while the most notable exception is the family. All the major branches of the Western Church are firmly established in the West Indies and their patterns of worship as well, as their beliefs and practices are very largely identical with those found in similar churches in this country. Thus, it would seem reasonable to expect that the churches here could provide, if not an 'open sesame' into wider society, at least a significant reference group with which the incoming migrant could be readily identified. In functional terms, one would expect the indigenous churches to be providing models of integration, which in time would lead to full assimilation and to similar acceptance in wider society. Such, however, has not been the case.[4]

4.8 Culture Shock

I went on to offer four reasons why West Indian migrants in the 1960s were not attending in Britain the same churches as they attended in the West Indies. The first was due to the culture shock of migration. The majority of the migrants had not come from the middle classes or the professions but from rural areas and from the peasant working class strata. The change to living in an urban industrialised white majority society was a radical culture shock. They had exchanged simple village life in an agrarian economy surrounded by supportive extended family patterns for a highly individualised, competitive and unfriendly society. Their daily experience was one of alienation and rejection and their tentative attempts to find support in local churches had been unsuccessful.

Secondly, I said that I saw the West Indians' rejection of the church in Britain as not being a rejection of their beliefs or of their traditional religious affiliations, but as a symbol of their disillusionment with, and disassociation from, the society and its culture which had rejected them. Thus, I believed that their rejection was socio-cultural rather than religious and this was a massive indictment of British churches.

4.9 Middle Class Institutions

Thirdly, I said that the English churches were largely middle class institutions enshrining middle class values. Studies of church attendance in working class areas in Victorian times, as E.R. Wickham said in his study of Sheffield,[5] showed that the church has never commanded the support of the working classes in Britain. But this is quite different from the situation in the West Indies where the churches *did* command the widespread support of the working classes. Hence, when the working class West Indian comes to Britain and goes to church, for the first time in his life he experiences a sense of social distance between himself and other members of the congregation. He feels shabbily dressed, poorly educated and at a grave social disadvantage in comparison with his middle class, socially secure white fellow worshippers. This, of course, was referring to the first generation of migrants in the 1950s and early 1960s. The situation is very different today.

4.10 Third Generation Theory

The fourth relevant factor I saw in terms of the 'Third Generation Theory',[6] in which the first generation simply look for a quiet life and seek social acceptance. The West Indians had recognised that the working classes who formed the majority of their neighbours and workmates did not go to church, so they accepted this as a rejection of institutional forms of Christianity in Britain. They had seen that if they did go to church they would increase their social distance and make acceptance in the local community more difficult.

4.11 Pentecostals

I also spoke about the Pentecostals who, throughout the 1960s, were enjoying enormous numerical success, not only in attracting former Pentecostals, but also those from traditional British denominations in the West Indies. I said:

> The success of the Pentecostals, wholly organised and led by immigrants, underlines the tragic failure of the traditional English churches to hold the allegiance of those immigrants who were already established Christians before coming to England. To see this failure in its true perspective one must bear in mind that in Jamaica, Pentecostals represent only 5% of the total Christian community.

I went on to outline three factors which accounted, at least in part, for the rapid growth of the immigrant Pentecostal congregations in Britain. The first was that, in the West Indies, most Pentecostal churches preached a doctrine of exclusive membership based upon strict observance of religious and ethical requirements. Sexual laxity was condemned; so were smoking, swearing, the use of makeup and any kind of adornment or artificial aids to beauty such as the straightening of the hair. The Pentecostals embraced a doctrine of conditional immortality based upon salvation through repentance and regeneration. They were very Bible-based, regarding themselves as the true believers, and that non-believers were destined for hell. In their home country they were used to being a 'separatist sect' and experiencing social rejection by wider society, so the experience of social rejection in Britain did not come as a shock to them. It was thus to be expected that their faith would have a higher survival rate than that of West Indians brought up in the traditional churches.

Secondly, the leaders of these immigrant churches had not only experienced rejection in wider society, but also within the English Pentecostal churches where they had not found acceptance. Within their meetings there was a flavour of nationalism and ethnocentrism which particularly appealed to the expatriate Jamaican. It was this element that also particularly appealed to non-Pentecostals who found consolation and support in the spiritual and social life of these church communities.

4.12 Millennialist Message

Thirdly, the preaching in the immigrant Pentecostal churches was strongly millennialist. Sermons usually emphasised the bad social conditions in Britain, the wickedness of wider society, rejection by society of the biblical values for which Pentecostals stood, and an 'otherworldly' message of salvation. Preachers emphasised the expectation of suffering in this life, but the hope of sudden divine intervention through the Second Coming of Christ, when those who were now suffering under the yoke of oppression will be justified and experience millennial joy in the presence of Messiah. This message accorded well with the daily life experience of the first generation of migrants and, no doubt, provided them with a degree of spiritual comfort which gave them fortitude in facing the trials and tribulations of life in Britain. It was very similar to the message of the missionaries under colonial slavery.

4.13 Second Generation

The message of the migrant Pentecostal churches, however, did not accord with the daily life experience of the second generation born in Britain and educated in schools alongside their white peer group. Their desire was for acceptance and integration into the host society. They were looking for immediate rewards rather than rewards in the afterlife. Thus the cultural gap between their daily life experience and what they were experiencing in their homes and in the migrant community associations of their parents was enormous. They reacted negatively against the strict disciplinarian culture of their parents and became rebellious rather than compliant. As soon as they were old enough they ceased going to church and they broke off contact with the community activities of their parents' generation.

The generation gap became a gulf that was almost unbridgeable. But it is this second generation who are the parents of the present generation of children and young people. It is they who have produced the generation involved in the riots of August 2011. It is therefore unsurprising that those young people who are raised in dysfunctional, chaotic families should react against a social environment that gives them no hope for the future in this life. Unless there are radical changes it is only a matter of time before another riot tears our inner-cities asunder.

4.14 Indictment of the Church

Looking back today in the aftermath of the 2011 riots, I have to say that as a nation we might never have reached this point if the white churches had responded to the immigration in accordance with the principles and beliefs of the Christian gospel. It grieves me to say this, but I know there were many churches where black faces were not welcome. This is something to which we must return in the final chapter.

Notes

[1] See press photograph of this in illustration section at end of book.

[2] See photograph in illustration section at end of book.

[3] Clifford Hill, *West Indian Migrants and the London Churches*, OUP, Oxford, 1963.

[4] Unpublished paper of speech made at this time.

[5] E R Wickham, *Church and People in an Industrial City*, Lutterworth Press, London, 1957.

[6] This is dealt with in Chapter 5.

Chapter Five

THIRD GENERATION THEORY

5.1 General Theory

In order to understand the social forces that have been at work in the immigrant communities since the early days of the post-war settlement of West Indian migrants in Britain, it is necessary to examine some sociological theoretical concepts. This will shed light on the transformation that has taken place, particularly in the social institution of family life. What was first known as the 'Third Generation Hypothesis' was developed by Will Herberg in 1960 from an original study of white immigrants in the USA.[1] It was later refined in a study in Detroit by Lazerwitz and Rowitz.[2] It is a useful sociological tool for analysing what has taken place in Britain since the 1950s in many inner-city areas of migrant settlement.

5.2 First Generation Migrants

The basic theory is that the first-generation migrants (here we are speaking of worker migrants rather than students) enter their country of adoption in order to improve their employment prospects and lifestyles through better work opportunities and better living conditions. They often send money home to support their families; and their socio/cultural centre remains in the country of origin.

These first-generation migrants have a limited desire for

integration and tend to form ethnic groups which maintain their cultural traditions. They have limited social or political ambitions so there is often no strong drive to overcome language or cultural barriers. This reinforces the desire to remain domiciled within the ethnic group and not to seek for social acceptance in wider society.

This tendency towards 'ghettoisation' creates problems for the children of first-generation migrants who, from the moment they enter nursery, playgroup or school, are forced to live in two worlds: the ethnic and that of the local children —their new peer group. The outcome is that immigrant children are inadequately socialised by their parents either in the local culture or in the ethnic culture. The result of this is the creation of a generation gap between parents and children which widens with age. By the time the children reach adolescence they may be in serious rebellion against the parents' ethnic culture which creates a range of social problems.

5.3 Second Generation Migrants

The second-generation migrants, who are the first generation to be born in the country of adoption, have very different objectives from their parents. Their aim is for full integration in the peer group culture and to make themselves fully acceptable with their local peer group. Their parents' home-land is a myth rather than a reality: it is part of the ethnic group mythology from which they wish to escape. For the second generation it exists only in the imaginary world of folk legend in their parents' generation.

The present reality for these children is the country of their birth, and it is their ambition to achieve in their birth country rather than in the unreal world of their parents. The ethnic group culture is often seen as a barrier to integration. For many this means rejecting the norms of the parents and adopting peer group norms which they see as essential to the achievement of their objectives. The reality is that few actually succeed in their socio-economic ambitions, which leaves the majority disappointed. The outcome is often a collective anomie that often characterises second-generation migrants who struggle with two cultural identities. This experience can go in one of two directions. If the individual is secure, and parents act wisely, he or she may achieve full integration into the host society and be successful in business and family life. But if this degree of integration is not achieved it may give rise to personality disorders, or to dysfunctional behavioural patterns.

5.4 Third Generation Migrants

The objectives of the third generation in the migrant community are very often determined by the experience of their parents. The third-generation children are no longer migrants. They are full citizens of the country where their grandparents chose to settle. If their parents have achieved full integration their children will often react against the local culture and seek to discover a distinctive identity by searching for their roots in their grandparents' homeland. This can also go in one of two ways. If the individual achieves socio-economic security, he or she is happy to display the distinctive cultural identity of their heritage while still playing a full part in the wider society. It is something of which they can boast, something that distinguishes them from everyone in the host society to which they belong, while still having a distinctive cultural identity torn from their grandparents' heritage. But if, on the other hand, the individual is insecure, or has inherited insecurity from a dysfunctional family life, the tendency is to reject the peer group culture and to look for security in traditional cultural groups, the outcome of which is alienation from and/or hostility towards wider society, or the adoption of in-group norms in a gang or sub-cultural group.

5.5 Summary

The Third Generation Theory states that the first generation of worker migrants are usually characterised by economic motives but a lack of socio/political ambition or expectations of social integration. They continue to identify with the culture and norms of their countries of origin.

The second generation seek full integration and therefore conform to the norms of the local peer group and tend to reject the culture of their parents' ethnic group.

The third generation, by contrast, if they are feeling secure in their peer group, will search for a distinctive identity in their family roots. If they are not securely integrated into the host society they will either react with alienation or hostility.

5.6 Additional Note

It is necessary to note that the theory was developed in America among *white migrants with European origins* and is only partially applicable to the British situation where ethnicity makes it impossible for migrants of African or Asian origin to merge indistinguishably in white majority British society, due to physical characteristics. However, the theory can be seen to be borne out to a limited extent among migrants from the UK whose work takes them to other countries such as India. Very rarely will the first generation merge with the local population but they will maintain a social distance, often sending their children back home to be educated, and often forming expatriate communities having only limited contact with the host population. If they settle on a permanent basis it is only their children — or grandchildren — who will achieve a degree of integration.

The Third Generation Theory has been tested in many

different migrant communities since the 1960s and it has been found to be a useful sociological tool for analysis of migrant community development. We are therefore applying it to the British situation while at the same time recognising the different variables that were not applicable to the original social situation when the theory was first used.

5.7 West Indian Migrants From 1948

First Generation Migrants
In the context of the limitations noted above of Third Generation Theory, it is now relevant to look at the situation of those whose origins are in the West Indian Islands. Many of the first group who came on the *Empire Windrush* in 1948, and others who came in the first wave of immigration, had served in the British Armed Forces during the Second World War. Having returned to their home environment where economic prosperity was limited, they decided to return to Britain, where prospects were much more advantageous. Their objectives were similar to most first-generation migrants in seeking better work and living conditions. They sent money home, not only for family support, but also to pay the fare of another family member to join them.

Their socio-cultural centre remained in their island origins, but ethnic groups and, later, Caribbean-led churches, formed important cultural centres and provided an expatriate support network. The migrants quickly adopted some of the norms of the local society, particularly in terms of family and marriage. Throughout the 1950s and 1960s, thousands of young couples married and set up house together. This contrasted only in age with Caribbean culture, where marriage was linked with socio-economic status and therefore was usually delayed until middle age (as we noted earlier).

The couples were soon able to earn considerably more

than they could in the Caribbean, and marriage marked their new socio-economic status. But in their ethnic culture, family and marriage were part of a matriarchal institution in which the grandmothers care for the upbringing of the children. This was rooted in slavery, where on many plantations marriage had been for some time forbidden to slaves under British colonial law.

Again as we saw, the grandmother culture developed strongly[3] after the abolition of the slave trade in 1807 when further imports of slaves from West Africa were illegal and the only source of additional labour was through population expansion. The strongest male slaves were encouraged to have as many children as possible, and the older women who were too weak to work in the field gangs became the child carers to the community. But in Britain there were no grandmothers, which put an inordinate strain upon the young mothers whose income was needed to meet the family budget and who struggled with the three roles — those of worker, mother and wife. The result was a high rate of family breakdown and many children being inadequately socialised. The outcome was a severe generation gap between parents and children.

Second Generation

The objective of the second-generation migrants is full integration with the peer group in the local communities where they had been born and where they went to school. For many there was a problem of identity. They were 'black' on the outside and 'white' inside. Their parents still related to the culture of the Caribbean Islands from which they had emigrated, but the culture, patois and mythology of the West Indies were alien to the children born in Britain.

They struggled with the two identities, and the desire for acceptance usually entailed rejection of the norms of their parents and the adoption of local peer group norms. For many of the second generation there was the additional struggle to attain educational qualifications in schools that were often part of the rundown inner-city environment where they grew up. It was an unequal struggle in which few succeeded in socio-economic terms. The outcome was a generation characterised by anomie.

Third Generation
In Britain we have now reached the third generation since the arrival of the first wave of post–World War II immigration that began with the *Empire Windrush* in 1948. This third generation of British African-Caribbeans struggle to discover a distinctive identity. Many of them come from broken families with insecure parents who have produced

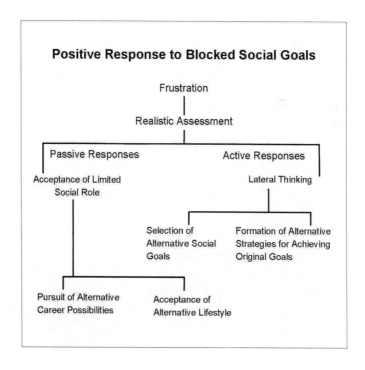

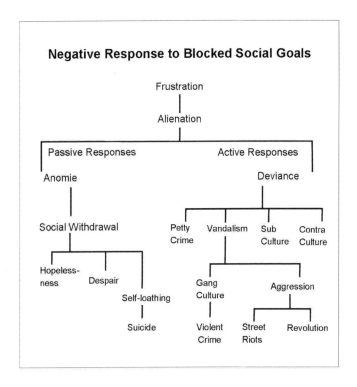

dysfunctional family homes. They are unsure of their own identity and lack a sense of purpose. Their parents are often unable to inspire them to achieve educational qualifications and gain social acceptance in the wider peer group culture. They do not have the desire, or see the need, to do so. Many of these parents do not value education and so do not feel the need to encourage their children to succeed. These parents are also unable to provide them with a sound and secure basis for personal and social morality.

This results in the formation of gangs as substitute families. The gang provides identity, a sense of belonging, security, protection and comfort. Many third-generation children reject the norms of what they see as a hostile society in which they cannot hope for social acceptance or economic achievement. The outcome is the formation of a counter-culture with its own 'in-group norms' and a form of alienation from wider society. The diagrams above show two contrasting models of the reaction to blocked social goals.

5.8 African Migrants From 1950

First Generation Migrants
Very few Africans came to Britain in the 1950s and 1960s. Those who came were mainly from West Africa. Many upper class families sent their children to Britain as students for advanced education. Their objectives were to gain educational qualifications and return to Africa. Most of them had no desire to settle in Britain and they returned to Africa where they formed a new educated professional middle class elite often locally known as the 'Been Tos' — those who had been to Europe for their further education.

Many of these professional elite were disappointed with the social and political situation in Africa. From the 1980s they began to return to Britain in considerable numbers or to send their children as first-generation migrants. Their cultural centre remained in their original African communities and the ethnic groups that have been created in Britain. African-led churches form an important part of the expatriate community and provide an opportunity to relax in congenial company, freed from the constraints of functioning in a society where acceptance is not guaranteed and in which cultural norms are not fully understood. This generation is mainly middle class, with leadership drawn from the professional classes. There is a high level of motivation, ambition and entrepreneurship, with strong desires for social integration and achievement ambitions for their children.

The largest of the African churches in Britain is the Redeemed Christian Church of God. They have churches in towns and cities throughout the UK. Twice yearly they hire the Excel Centre in east London for an all-night prayer meeting that begins at 8.00 p.m. on a Friday night and goes right through until 6.00 a.m. on Saturday morning. Their numbers have steadily increased since the year 2000, and in 2010 each of their two meetings was attended by 50,000 adherents. This level of attendance has been maintained in the years 2011 and 2012.

For several years their young people met in a separate hall until in 2009, when the 5,000-strong gathering of young people was invaded by a local East End gang complaining that they were on their 'turf'. The ensuing melee had to be broken up by staff and police, which resulted in the Excel Centre authorities banning the separate meeting of young people, who now have to merge with the adult meeting. The meetings themselves are not entirely for prayer, but also provide opportunities for worship, choral singing, items of music that appeal to the largely Nigerian gathering. The meetings provide a unique opportunity for Africans to celebrate their culture and to meet with their friends as well as seek spiritual consolation and strength through their faith in God.

Second Generation Migrants
The objectives of this second generation who are first-generation Africans born in Britain is full integration with their local peer group. Many, however, are unsure of their identity growing up in two cultures—the world of their parents, which is part of the ethnic mythology from which they try to distance themselves in the transition from childhood to adolescence, and the world of school and local peer group norms which become increasingly important to them.

Like the second generation of Caribbean children, they

too suffer the role conflict of being black on the outside and white inside. They know that if they are to achieve in socio-economic terms in wider society they have to conform to the norms of that society. Many of them have parents who are highly ambitious for their children and put pressures upon them to succeed in obtaining educational qualifications which will lead to professional careers.

There are several factors that militate against educational attainment. These are:

- If they are living in a working class area, the schools may not be of a particularly high standard.
- The local working class norms do not encourage academic success.
- They are influenced by Black British culture which has largely been formed by the Caribbean second and third generations whose counter-culture norms are contrary to academic success.
- A fourth factor that creates difficulty for African migrants is that most British people do not make any distinction between Africans and Caribbeans. Many British people think they all look alike and this is deeply offensive to most Africans whose culture is quite different from that of the West Indian Islands.

The outcome for many of these young people is a struggle to find their identity in a clash of cultures. On the one hand there is the desire to please parents, or at least not to incur the wrath of parents, and on the other hand the desire for peer group acceptance. In many ways their situation is more difficult than that of the Caribbeans because their ethnic culture is patriarchal in contrast to the Caribbean matriarchal family type, and it is authoritarian rather than libertarian. The pressures upon these young people can therefore often be intense, leading to depression or ill-health.

5.9 Asian Migrants since 1960

First Generation

There is no such thing as a homogeneous Asian migrant community in Britain. The differences between Pakistanis, Indians, Bangladeshis, Chinese and others from the Asian continent are great in terms not only of nationality but religion, language and culture. For our present purpose, we will simply focus upon the Pakistani community, who are the most numerous of the Asian migrant communities in Britain. The application of Third Generation Theory to the Pakistani community produces some interesting conclusions. In a similar way to the West Indians, Pakistanis in Britain have now reached their third generation. Very few came in the 1950s but once they began coming in 1960 they very soon numerically outstripped migrants from the West Indies. In fact it was the potential of millions of Indians and Pakistanis coming to Britain that triggered the Commonwealth Immigrants Act of 1962. The first generation, as was to be expected, made very little attempt at any socio/political activity. They were content to find work and accommodation wherever they could and to send support to their relatives at home.

Second Generation

This second generation sought integration and acceptance in the predominantly white host society with whom they were educated. The tightly controlled organisation of family life in the Pakistani migrant communities, however, militated strongly against this integration. Religion and culture were the dominant factors, and the formation of mosques with Pakistani Imams, who spoke very little English and who exercised considerable influence in the community, played a significant part in preventing integration of the second generation. The Imams insisted on the children attending extracurricular classes for learning Arabic and being taught the Qur'an. This placed a considerable strain upon the children after a full day at school, but the strict discipline within the family made it impossible for them to drop out. Attendance at these classes, however, prevented Pakistani children from playing with other children in the neighbourhood and curtailed their cross-cultural social intercourse.

Third Generation

The third generation who, according to Third Generation Theory would normally be seeking their roots, had no opportunity of avoiding their roots! Those roots formed their whole social environment. Theirs was, in fact, a world-denying existence. Large numbers of girls every year are sent back to Pakistan for arranged marriages with partners from cultures that are totally alien to girls educated in Britain, which often result in great suffering and stress for those involved. There is a high rate of marriage breakdown in these partnerships, which adds to the tensions within the Pakistani migrant communities where family loyalty and honour are highly valued.

There are even greater tensions among boys who are educated alongside white boys immersed in twenty-first century British youth culture. The culture of the first and second generations is a strong influence in the third generation, but they lack the security of integration into the host society. They are socially alienated. Instead, they are surrounded by a culture that engenders hostility towards the host society and the rejection of all the social values of that society. This can easily lead to hatred and even to violent opposition among those who are insecure, such as is seen in street demonstrations or terrorist activity.

5.10 The Problem Facing Parents

The core of the problem facing parents of all ethnic backgrounds today is not racial or ethnic in essence. It is a clash of cultures and it needs to be understood in this context if parenting is to be successful, and if young people are to survive the traumas of adolescence and become well-adjusted young adults. This clash of cultures is not confined to the children of immigrants. It is also experienced by Christian families living in inner-city areas who have different family values from the prevailing culture. For the children of black immigrants it is intensified by their physical appearance, which automatically associates them with the non-white sector and may be a hindrance to full integration in the host society.

In terms of the clash of cultures I can speak from personal experience as I have spent many years in inner-city areas of London. My wife and I have pastored churches in Harlesden (west London), Tottenham (north London), Newham (east London) and in Lambeth (south London) — all ethnically mixed, working class inner-city places, with all the problems that characterise these kinds of area. All our three children were born and grew up where we lived, and we often wept for our children, especially in their struggles to cope with the inadequate educational facilities in local schools. We were there because we believed we were called to live and work there but our children had no choice. They had to interact in the local culture and to make their friendships with local children who often came from families with values very different from our own.

We were able to supplement their schooling, which enabled each of them to obtain a university education, but we constantly talked to our children and discussed the difference between the biblically-based Christian values in our family and those they encountered in the neighbourhood.

We discovered that this openness worked well, and that with the strong support of a stable and caring home life our children were able to cope with living in two contrasting cultures. Family prayers helped to strengthen them for the situations they had to face in daily life. All three not only survived but are now in professional occupations and in secure and loving marriages.

Parents whose children are encountering a culture clash need to understand the pressures upon their children and to be wise enough to know when to be firm and when to relax. Family time together is precious, and open discussion of the contrasting values of the family and those of wider society is absolutely essential if parents are to have the joy of seeing their children grow into mature adults. It is a challenge, but it can be done!

Notes

[1] Will Herberg, *Protestant, Catholic, Jew. An essay in American Religious Sociology,* Garden City, New York, Doubleday, 1955.

[2] Lazerwitz and Rowitz, *The Three Generations Hypothesis*, American Journal of Sociology, University of Chicago Press, 1964.

[3] It became institutionalised, particularly in rural working class culture, after the emancipation of slaves in 1838.

Chapter Six

COLONIAL SLAVERY AND
THE TRADE TRIANGLE

"As soon as slavery is mentioned,
all the black kids' heads go down"
— London schoolteacher

6.1 Slave Ship Exhibition

The year 2007 marked the 200th anniversary of the abolition
of the European slave trade between Africa and the Americas.
The trade had existed for 300 years and, following a twenty
year campaign in Parliament led by William Wilberforce, it
was abolished in the year 1807. As part of the anniversary
commemorations, my wife and I led a team that mounted an
exhibition of colonial slavery at All Hallows by the Tower
in the City of London.[1] We set up a piece of research using
questionnaires which were completed by 6,000 members
of the public who attended the exhibition. There was a
remarkable lack of knowledge about colonial slavery in
the British Empire. Only 9% of the white British people
attending claimed to have 'a good knowledge' of the subject;
28% said that they had a little knowledge, but 63% said they
had no knowledge of the subject.

These respondents were all people who had taken the
trouble to visit an exhibition of colonial slavery and had paid
for entry. It would be reasonable to conclude, therefore, that
they had an interest in the subject, and therefore that even

less than 9% of the general public had any knowledge at that time of the 300-year period of British colonial slavery. It is a large period in our history that is entirely unknown to the vast majority of the British population. That would still be true today of the adult population because the subject of slavery did not feature in the curriculum of state schools in Britain before 2007, so anyone whose formal school education finished before that year would not have been taught about slavery unless they went to one of the more enlightened private schools, a few of which did some teaching on the subject.

6.2 Victims and Oppressors

One of the first teachers to teach this subject in a state school spoke to me after her first few weeks' experience. She works in an area of London where there is a large community with West Indian backgrounds. She said, "It's a strange thing, but as soon as I begin to speak about slavery, all the black kids' heads go down." I asked her why she thought this happened. She said that it was clear to her that the black kids all felt ashamed of their background. I said, "But this is surely turning justice upside down! It was the black kids' ancestors who were the *victims* of oppression. Surely it should have been the white kids whose heads went down because it was their ancestors who were the *oppressors*!" She agreed, "Perhaps," she said, "It's like the women who are too ashamed to go to the police when they've been raped. But I'm simply telling you what happens in the classroom."

Why should this happen? Why should such a reversal of justice take place? What makes the black kids feel ashamed of their own history? It is surely part of the legacy of slavery that still exists in our society today. It is a reflection of the deeply rooted attitudes to black people that still exist today among white people and have their effect upon black people.

The roots lie in colonial slavery where all the records show that the Europeans regarded the African people as a lower order of humanity. That attitude was actually institutionalised in both Britain and America for hundreds of years. In Britain the first legislation to make the public expression of racism illegal was in the second half of the twentieth century — in the lifetime of most people still living. But changes in the law only slowly affect attitudes, and the continuing existence of latent racist opinions is undeniable, as is amply illustrated at some football matches where racist comments are still shouted at black footballers despite the strong action of the Football Association.

6.3 US Constitution

In the USA, the American people won their independence from Britain in 1776. Having successfully won freedom from British rule, they were then faced with a quandary because this freedom could not be granted to all its human constituents without destroying a major part of its existing socio-economic structure — slavery played an important part in the life and economy of the nation, especially in the southern States. In drawing up the National Constitution, the Founding Fathers of the USA faced this problem, which they solved by doing a headcount of all the so-called 'free persons' (who were the white population) and then adding 'three-fifths of the total of all the other persons'. This, of course, was a euphemism for those Africans who were 'slaves'. These were people living in States who had just been freed from British rule, but each slave only counted as 'three-fifths of a person' in the Constitution of the USA.

The United States of America, at its foundation, therefore recognised slavery as an integral part of its existence. This, in effect, institutionalised a racist definition of all people of African descent, a label that was to last for two hundred years, being still active at the time of Martin Luther King, who led the campaign for freedom and equality in the 1960s. Thus the personal freedom created by the US Constitution was both partial and selective, placing Africans in a socially inferior position. This position survived the nineteenth century abolition of slavery. African people were free in the law, but not in the eyes of the master race where attitudes ignored the law, and segregation existed in education, on public transport, in employment, and in many other spheres of life. It was real and actual although illegal. There is still today a legacy of slavery in the USA, although it is different from that in Britain where slavery has been declared illegal since 1771, and there has never been a large black slave population.

6.4 Immigration Act 1596
In Britain, although there are similarities, the historical situation is different. It is worth noting that the Commonwealth Immigrants Act 1962, which was passed in the reign of Queen Elizabeth II, was not the first on the statute book of Britain to limit the flow of black people into this country. The first was some four hundred years earlier, in the reign of Queen Elizabeth I. In 1596 a similar measure was passed.

> Her Majesty, understanding that there are of late divers black–mores brought into this realme, of which kinde of people there are already too manie, consideringe howe God hath blessed this land with great increase of people of our owne nation...those kinde of people should be sent forth of the lande.[2]

In the eighteenth century many wealthy families who owned plantations in the West Indies and America often brought black slaves to serve in their households in Britain. In fact it became quite fashionable in London and other large cities to have Africans in attendance as personal servants. This practice was not approved by everyone as was expressed by a writer in *The Gentleman's Magazine* of 1764. He wrote:

> The practice of importing negro servants into these kingdoms is said to be already a grievance that requires a remedy, and yet it is everyday encouraged, insomuch that the number in this Metropolis only, is supposed to be near 20,000; the main objection to their importation is that they cease to consider themselves as slaves in this free country, nor will they put up with an inequality of treatment, nor more willingly perform the laborious duties of servitude than our own people, and if put to it, are generally sullen, spiteful, treacherous and revengeful. It is therefore highly impolitic to introduce them as servants here where that rigour and severity is impracticable, which is absolutely necessary to make them useful.[3]

6.5 Slavery Illegal in Britain

Just seven years after the publication of this statement, slavery was established as illegal in Britain by the 1771 Mansfield Declaration. This was the outcome of a case brought by Granville Sharp, one of the early abolitionists who had befriended an African slave who had been ill-treated by his master. Sharp had found him in a London street, deeply distressed and physically near to death. He had cared for him and restored him to health. Then his erstwhile master who had cruelly treated him recognised him in London and reclaimed him. Sharp brought the issue before the court and judgement was given by Lord Chief Justice Mansfield that slavery was illegal in England. This judgement given by Lord Mansfield was that anyone who set foot on English soil was immediately free. The judgement had some unforeseen outcomes as about 14,000 slaves were set free and many of them were unable to find employment and were soon reduced to absolute poverty. It became a common sight in London to see black beggars, and several hundred of them made a personal appeal to Granville Sharp for assistance, which resulted in the formation of a 'Committee for Relieving the Black Poor'. The idea was conceived of establishing a colony for these unfortunates in Sierra Leone. It was an idea that appealed to both the abolitionists and the Government. The abolitionists saw it as a means of demonstrating that Africans could develop a Christian civilisation which would be a model on that continent. The Government simply saw it as a means of getting rid of an awkward problem and willingly gave financial aid in order to clear the streets of London and relieve it of some embarrassment.

The fact that slavery had been officially declared illegal in Britain in no way affected the attitudes of those who financially benefited from colonial slavery. The twenty year parliamentary battle to end the slave trade is a testimony to the dedication of a handful of abolitionists who persevered in the face of powerful vested interests which were represented in both Houses of Parliament. The battle effectively began on Sunday 28 October 1787, when William Wilberforce wrote in his diary, 'God Almighty has set before me two great objects, the suppression of the slave trade and the reformation of manners' [moral values].

6.6 Abolition Campaign

Wilberforce actually reversed the chronology of these two objectives by persuading the King to sponsor a movement for the 'Suppression of Vice and Immorality' before he threw his energies into the abolition of the slave trade. In his mind the two objects were always interconnected. He saw slavery primarily as a moral issue. He hated all forms of cruelty and violence and he was one of the founders of the Royal Society for the Prevention of Cruelty to Animals (RSPCA).

His focus was consistently upon reforming the moral values of the nation, an important part of which was the abolition of slavery in the colonies, and the relief of suffering and oppression among the industrial poor in Britain.

It was the cruelty and dehumanising effect of slavery that was the prime motivation behind the drive for abolition, led by Wilberforce and the Clapham Group of evangelical Christian social reformers. The group included some remarkable men and at least one woman, Hannah More, whose dedication to providing education for the poor was unparalleled. Granville Sharp, Thomas Clarkson, and Zachary Macaulay, each with their different gifts, formed a small team who were tireless researchers and campaigners. They provided a wealth of empirical evidence which was not only invaluable to the Parliamentary campaign, but eventually became a powerful instrument for influencing public opinion.

Thomas Clarkson was unstinting in providing Wilberforce with evidence of the monstrous inhumanity of the slave trade. On one occasion he sought a sailor whom he needed as an eyewitness. He had seen him once, but he did not know the man's name. He systematically searched ships from one port to another until he found him on the 317th ship he visited. That is dedication!

6.7 Wilberforce

Wilberforce made good use of the evidence that his researchers presented to him. In his first speech in the House of Commons introducing a motion on the 12 May 1789 for the abolition of the slave trade, Wilberforce used all his eloquence and powers of persuasion, which can be seen even today from the following extracts from Hansard:

When I consider the magnitude of the subject which I am to bring before the house – a subject, in which the interests, not of this country, nor of Europe alone, but of the whole world, and of posterity, are involved: and when I think, at the same time, on the weakness of the advocate who has undertaken this great cause – when these reflections press upon my mind, it is impossible for me not to feel both terrified and concerned at my own inadequacy to such a task.

But when I reflect, however, on the encouragement which I have had, through the whole course of a long and laborious examination of this question, how much candour I have experienced, and how much conviction has increased within my own mind, in proportion as I have advanced in my labours; when I reflect, especially that however adverse any gentleman may now be, yet we shall all be of one opinion in the end; – when I turn myself to these thoughts, I take courage – I determine to forget all my other fears, and I march forward with a firmer step in the full assurance that my cause will bear me out, and that I shall be able to justify, upon the clearest principles, every resolution in my hand, the avowed end of which is, the total abolition of the slave trade...

I mean not to accuse anyone, but to take the shame upon myself, in common, indeed, with the whole Parliament of Great Britain, for having suffered this horrid trade to be carried on under their authority. We are all guilty – we ought all to plead guilty and not to exculpate ourselves by throwing the blame on others; and I therefore deprecate every kind of reflection against the various descriptions of people who are more immediately involved in this wretched business.[4]

6.8 Trade Triangle

Wilberforce described some of the appalling conditions on the slave ships during the infamous second leg of the Trade Triangle, the passage across the Atlantic with Africans packed like cattle into overloaded ships. He then went on to deal with the charge that abolition would ruin the economy of the West Indies, the livelihoods of the colonists and those in Britain who depended upon the trade. There were also great fears that, once the slaves were released from the harsh discipline on the plantations, the whites would all be murdered. He said that he was prepared to "prove, by authentic evidence, that, in truth, the West Indies have nothing to fear from the total and immediate abolition of the slave trade." He was deeply concerned about the terrible harm that the slave trade had done to Africa in degrading the people and encouraging "brutishness and barbarity". In the same speech he said:

Let us then make such amendments as we can for the mistakes we have done to that unhappy continent: let us recollect what Europe itself was no longer ago than three or four centuries. What if I should be able to show this house that in a civilised part of Europe in the time of our Henry VII there were people who actually sold their own children? What if I should tell them that England itself was that country? What if I should point out to them that the very place where this inhuman traffic was carried on, was the city of Bristol?

Ireland at that time used to drive a considerable trade in slaves with these neighbouring barbarians; but a great plague having infested the country, the Irish were struck with a panic, suspected (I am sure very properly) that the plague was a punishment sent from heaven, for the sin of the slave trade, and therefore abolished it. All I ask, therefore, of the people of Bristol, is, that they should become as civilised now as the Irishmen were 400 years ago.

In his final appeal to Parliament, Wilberforce said:

Sir, the nature and all the circumstances of this trade are now laid open to us; we can no longer plead ignorance... It is brought now so directly before our eyes, that this House must decide, and must justify to all the world, and to their own consciences, the rectitude of the grounds and principles of their decision. A society has been established for the abolition of this trade in which Dissenters, Quakers, churchmen... have all united... Let not Parliament be the only body that is insensible to the principles of national justice. Let us make reparation to Africa... and we shall soon find rectitude of our conduct rewarded by the benefits of a regular and growing commerce.[5]

Eloquence was not sufficient to overcome the vested interests of wealth which were dependent upon the prosperity of the plantations. Year after year Wilberforce introduced another Abolition Bill, and each time it was defeated. In 1792 he detailed the horrors of the trade, speaking of ship after ship, which set out from Africa loaded with healthy young Africans of whom up to half were likely to die before they reached the Americas or the Indies in up to three months of hell in ships that were entirely dependent upon the wind and the prevailing weather conditions. They were housed on shelves manacled in pairs, packed so tightly together that they could scarcely breathe. Olaudah Equiano, one of the outstanding African abolitionists, who had been captured as a small child and experienced the horrors of transportation across the Atlantic, described the scene in this way:

The stench of the hold while we were on the coast was so intolerably loathsome, that it was dangerous to remain there for any time... Some of us were permitted to stay on deck for the fresh air: but now that the whole ship's cargo were confined together, it became absolutely pestilential. The closeness of the place and the heat of the climate added to the number in the ship almost suffocated us. This produced copious perspiration, so that the air soon became unfit for respiration, from a variety of loathsome smells, and brought on a sickness among the slaves, of which many died, thus falling victims to the greed of their purchasers.[6]

Similar conditions were described by John Newton, who was himself a former slave ship captain before joining the growing company of abolitionists. He wrote:

The slave ship captain will try to take as many as possible. The cargo of a vessel of 100 tons can hold between 220 and 250 slaves. Their lodging rooms below the deck, which are three (for the men, the boys and women) besides a place for the sick, are sometimes more than 5 feet high, and sometimes less; and this height is divided towards the middle, the slaves lying in two rows, one above the other, on the side of the ship, close to each other, like books upon a shelve. I have known them so close, that the shelf would not easily have contained one more.

The poor creatures, thus cramped for want of room, are likewise in irons, for the most part both hands and feet, and two together, which makes it difficult for them to turn or move, to attempt either to rise or to lie down, without hurting themselves, or each other. The heat and smell of these rooms, added to the galling of their irons, and the depression which seizes their spirits, soon becomes fatal.[7]

In his 1792 speech in the House of Commons Wilberforce gave a horrifying description of the slave trade that shocked the House. He described the case of a young girl of fifteen who had evidently resisted the desires of the captain on board a slave ship. He tied her by her wrists and beat her, then tied her by her legs and beat her. Not content with this, he finally tied her by one leg, raising her on the mast and beat her until she died. The debate in the Commons went on right through the night, with both Prime Minister Pitt and Leader of the Opposition Fox adding their weight in favour of abolition but all was in vain, the power of vested interests prevailed. The word 'gradually' had been introduced as an amendment. The House seized upon this to ease the troubled consciences of Members. They were able to agree that the trade should be stopped — but only gradually, with no date given. It actually took another fifteen years before the trade was finally abolished.

6.9 The Zong

It was, however, the case of the *Zong,* the most notorious of the eighteenth century slave ships, that defined the position of African slaves in British law, and established the status of black people in the eyes of the white population of Britain. The legacy, in the form of remnants of that status, lingered on right into the decade of the 1960s. This was amply demonstrated in the abusive and racist attacks that came through my letterbox in the early 1960s.[8]

The *Zong* was a slave ship that came to prominence in Britain through a disputed insurance claim between Gregson, its Liverpool owner (former Lord Mayor of Liverpool) and the insurance underwriters. The *Zong* sailed from the West Coast of Africa on 6 September 1781, with a cargo of 470 Africans bound for Jamaica. Three months later the ship lost its way in the Caribbean Sea adding to the distress of all on board, where there was severe malnutrition and sickness. On 29 November, Captain Collingwood called the crew together saying that their fresh water supply was rapidly dwindling and if they were to survive the journey they needed to reduce the number of slaves on board. Sixty of the Africans and seven of the seventeen-man crew had already died on the journey.

He proposed throwing overboard those who were sick, explaining that under British insurance law, "If the slaves died a natural death, it would be the loss of the owners of the ship; but if they were thrown alive into the sea, it would be the loss of the underwriters." There can be no doubt that his real motivation was economic greed. Most of the Africans, after so long at sea, were in a very poor physical condition. He knew that they would probably not have fetched a good price on the slave market in Kingston, Jamaica. But under British maritime insurance law, each of the live Africans thrown overboard on the justification of saving the lives of the remainder, and of the crew, would fetch £30.

Heavy rain fell about this time, which gave them plenty of fresh water and when the *Zong* finally landed in Jamaica on 22 December it had 420 gallons of water on board. Nevertheless, the crew selected those who were sick, and the first batch of 54 live Africans were thrown overboard on 29 November, followed a few days later by another batch of 42, and soon after that another 26 were thrown into the sea with their manacles still attached. A further 10 were said to have jumped overboard when witnessing the fate of the others, making a total of 132 deliberately drowned at the whim of the captain. What happened to Captain Luke Collingwood is unknown, but he did not survive the journey and is thought to have died in Jamaica. Certainly he was not available to give evidence in the court case brought by the owners against the insurance underwriters for their refusal to pay compensation for the drowned slaves.

6.10 Olaudah Equiano and Granville Sharp

It was the former slave, Olaudah Equiano, who drew the attention of Granville Sharp to this infamous case and he decided to rally support for a prosecution of the *Zong's* crew. Before he could take such an action, the underwriters, who had lost the first hearing against them, lodged an appeal which came before Lord Justice Mansfield in May 1783. The slave ship owners were represented by the Solicitor General, John Lee, who said that the master of the ship had an unquestioned right to throw overboard as many Africans as he wished without "any shew or suggestion of cruelty, or a surmise of impropriety." Seeing Granville Sharp in the public gallery drew from Lee the following infamous statement. He said:

"What is all this vast declaration of human beings thrown overboard?

The question after all, is, was it voluntary, or an act of necessity? This is a case of chattels or goods. It is really so: it is the case of throwing over goods; for to this purpose, and the purpose of the insurance, they are goods and property: whether right or wrong, we have nothing to do with it. This property — the human creatures if you will — have been thrown overboard: whether or not for the preservation of the rest, that is the real question."[9]

In his summing up, Lord Mansfield reminded the jury that they had to deal with this case in terms of insurance law, not on any other grounds and that the slaves were goods, the property of the owners. He said that: "In the case of the slaves, it was the same as if horses had been thrown overboard." Granville Sharp tried to persuade his friends in the Government to get involved and to bring charges against the crew for acts of murder. But although the case aroused a great deal of public sympathy and expressions of outrage, it was perfectly clear that if this case were pursued through the courts it would undermine the whole institution of colonial slavery, which was based upon the right of Europeans to own the Africans as property. Their status was not that of human beings but as chattels. That was the whole basis, not only of the trade but of the social organisation of the colonies in the Americas.

This status was actually defined by an Act of Parliament in London in 1790 in a clause regulating insurance, which said: 'No loss or damage shall be recoverable on account of the mortality of slaves by natural death or ill-treatment, or against loss by throwing overboard of slaves on any account whatsoever.' Commenting on this, James Walvin, in *Black Ivory*, [10] wrote:

Parliament felt obliged to legislate because slaves continued to be killed on English slave ships. It had been apparent for many years that the English slave trade was built on violence. It was not simply that slaves died because of haphazard freaks of circumstance, by the accident of fate, by illness, misfortune, or at the hands of vicious (if untypical) slave traders; it was abundantly clear that the slave trade was a system conceived, sustained and nurtured by interrelated systems of violence.... Everyone involved in the slave trade had a keen interest in keeping slaves alive; equally, they were willing to kill and to inflict injury if necessary. *To kill a slave, or a group of slaves, was an economic misfortune, but it did not constitute a human outrage which offended or worried those involved.*[11] [My italics]

6.11 Plantation Slavery

Walvin is right in saying that the whole institution of slavery was based upon violence. It was a lucrative business for the perpetrators, beginning with the Arab raiders who captured people in their village communities and force marched them to the west coast of Africa, where they were sold to African traders, who in turn sold them to European sailors for transportation to the Americas. Once they reached the plantations, the African slaves, who had already lost their freedom, lost everything else that pertained to human rights and personal dignity. They were not only forced to work in the cruellest and most degrading circumstances, but they were also robbed of their language, their culture, their names and their identity. They were punished for speaking their native tongues and forced to speak English. They were branded with the name of their owner, or the name of the estate. Their own African name was lost forever and they were given the name of the estate owner — they were his property.

African family life was fatally damaged by the experience of plantation slavery. Even if Africans of similar tribal and language groups were shipped together on the voyage across the Atlantic, the slave market would distribute them to various plantations across the island where they were at the mercy of their white masters, who used the women to indulge their sexual appetites. The inevitable fruit of such liaisons changed the course of social history in the West Indian territories. It produced a complex system of social differentiation in which light-coloured offspring were granted preferential treatment. This gradually evolved into the variegated colour class system which had developed by the time of emancipation and still exists today.

Slave women could achieve better lifestyles for themselves and enhance the prospects of their children by relationships with white men. By 1833 the population in the British Caribbean islands was 16,000 whites, 310,000 slaves, but also a substantial population of 31,000 coloured. These last enjoyed a special position in society, where lighter skin and more European features led to automatic social preference and eventual freedom.

These relationships had a profound effect upon family life which is still influential today. During the twenty years of Parliamentary abolition debates MPs were often appalled by the accounts of sexual laxity and licence. Slave women were entirely at the disposal of their white masters and were often offered casually to visiting friends, with beatings and punishments when sexual advances were resisted. This situation existed right across the Caribbean and North and South America wherever African slaves were introduced.

> Slaves were there to do as the white man bid, they were to obey his
> sexual as much as his labouring instructions. Yet it was one of slavery's
> greatest ironies that white 'justification' for the rapacious use of slave
> women was the traditional or even 'natural' promiscuity of the blacks.
> (Walvin *op. cit.*, p. 191)

The injustice of slavery reached outrageous proportions

by this justification of the white men's sexual exploitation of the African women by declaring that it was their fault. It was a case of the victim being blamed for the sins of the oppressor. In the early days of the slave trade, men greatly outnumbered the women, so it was not uncommon for groups of men to roam through the slave estate compounds looking for sexual satisfaction, which led to the planters importing more women. But stable family life under colonial slavery was impossible as the slaves were entirely at the disposal of those in charge of the estates, and African men and women could both be sold and moved to other estates regardless of their family liaisons. After the end of the slave trade in 1807 it was common policy of the estates to encourage the strongest males to produce as many babies as possible in order to continue the supply of labour. This encouraged the casual but unstable relationships among young adults which became institutionalised by the time full emancipation was reached some thirty years later. A contemporary 1823 account of life in Jamaica reported:

> The husband has commonly two or three wives, and the wives as many husbands which they mutually change for each other.[12]

The patterns of unstable family life which were apparent at the time of my visit to Jamaica in the 1960s undoubtedly had their roots in plantation slavery and it was inevitable that these socio-cultural traditions were transported to Britain with the first wave of immigration. The enthusiasm for marriage which I encountered among the first generation of migrants in the 1950s and early 60s did not last long. It was not only the difficulties they encountered, but the impact of the changing culture in Britain of the 1960s and 70s was influential in changing attitudes among the settlers which added to the instability of family life.

6.12 Loss of African Identity

Many West Indian immigrants, and their descendants in Britain today, still deeply resent their loss of African identity. They see this as part of the ongoing legacy of slavery. If they seek to trace their roots, which is one of the aspirations of third generation immigrants, they are unable to get farther back than the sugar plantations on which their forebears were enslaved in the Caribbean. It is impossible even to find which part of Africa they came from, or their tribal identity, owing to the movement of slaves from one plantation to another. Some see the English name they bear as a continuation of the system of branding inflicted upon their forefathers. Their African names have been lost, as finally as the 1,300,000 Africans were lost in the Atlantic on the second leg of the Trade Triangle.

In their search for identity and communal dignity, many West Indians take some comfort in the struggle for freedom of the Africans in the Americas and in the West Indian islands. They often resent the European emphasis upon the white heroes of abolition, such as Wilberforce, and members of the Clapham Group of reformers, while scant attention is paid to the resistance of the Africans themselves, who played a large part in the final achievement of their freedom.

Without the writings of Equiano and Cuguano, without Toussaint, Louverture and Moyse, Christophe and Dessalines, Pierrot and Goman, Julien Fedon, Padilla and Romero, Jordan and Sharpe, Mary Prince, Bissette and Pory Pappy, Petion and Buddhoe and so many other black rebels and abolitionists, the challenge to colonial slavery could not have triumphed. The escalating slave resistance in Barbados in 1816, Guyana in 1823 and Jamaica 1831–2 achieved both a larger scale and more intimate engagement with the slave regime than any previous revolts in the British Caribbean. They were also more clearly aimed at contesting the whole slave system.[13]

It is of enormous importance for the future of community relationships in Britain that the contribution of these Africans in the abolition of colonial slavery is recognised. They have never been honoured by British historians who champion the names of Wilberforce, Thornton, Macaulay, Hannah More, Granville Sharp, John Newton, Buxton and many more, but rarely mention the names of the African heroes, some of whom paid with their lives in the struggle for abolition. This adds to the sense of injustice and convinces those of African descent who are now part of British society that attitudes have not changed.

6.13 End of Slavery

It is also of historical significance that the role of the Maroons in harassing the plantocracy should not be ignored. They were a constant threat to the dominant white minority in Jamaica and played a significant part in persuading the plantation owners to accept the inevitable when the Abolition of Slavery Bill was finally passed in Westminster in 1833. But the part played by these African rebels has never been acknowledged as part of the struggle against slavery.

Many West Indians in London were unhappy when shown a preview of the film 'Amazing Grace' in 2006. They saw it as yet another piece of white superiority, ignoring the role of the Black abolitionists. They also resented the film ending on a note of triumphalism hailing Wilberforce as the great hero, which they saw as yet another instance of white paternalism and the white man's interpretation of history to his own advantage.

Inevitably, there are different views and interpretations of the evidence of the fifty-year movement for the abolition of slavery. At one extreme there are those who believe that abolition was achieved on purely humanitarian grounds, led by white politicians and social reformers with the aid of one or two black activists. At the other extreme there is the view of Dr Eric Williams, former Prime Minister of Trinidad, who said that slavery was becoming uneconomic and was abolished purely on economic grounds. No doubt his personal Marxist philosophy led him to such a conclusion on grounds of economic determinism, but the evidence does not support this view.

Of course, the work of Wilberforce and his friends was essential because it was only the rich who were able to become Members of Parliament. They held all the power, but it would be wrong to say that theirs was the only influence that brought about the end of slavery. The increasing resistance and unrest among the slaves undoubtedly played a significant part in persuading the plantation owners that it was in their long-term interests to accept the emancipation package.

There is a further reason for the importance of recognising the role of the Africans themselves in the abolition movement. It is not only historically significant, but it also has great social significance, particularly for those whose forebears were the victims of slavery. The effect of colonial slavery was not only to dehumanise, but to destroy every semblance of personal dignity of the slaves. Therefore, to recognise the important role that they themselves exercised in their own liberation is a vital element in dealing with the legacy of slavery. Such recognition by white historians would go a long way towards combating the low self-image and low self-esteem of the descendants of the West Indian Africans. This recognition would not be an act of charity, but an act of *justice*—of setting the record straight.

If slavery were properly taught in schools, the situation described at the beginning of this chapter would not occur. Truth and justice demand that the full story of the abolition of colonial slavery is made known, not only to the third generation of West Indian children in Britain today, but to their white peer group. This would be an important step towards reconciliation and dealing with the problems of low self-image among young people in inner-city areas of social deprivation. It is important to recognise that social deprivation is not necessarily economic but may also be a product of injustice.

There is still a great reluctance among British politicians to say anything that amounts to an apology for colonial slavery in case it carries implications of the current British Government accepting responsibility for what happened two hundred and more years ago. It would not be difficult today to find a majority of politicians who would agree that the terms of the emancipation in 1833 were not only grossly unfair to the slaves but they were an obscene injustice too. In awarding £20 million to the planters and not a penny to the African victims of slavery, the British Government was actually perpetuating the role of slavery by paying the owners for the loss of their 'property'. Thus, although they were set free, they had no means to support themselves and they found themselves in a social situation in which they had no defined position and were still largely at the mercy of those who owned the land.

Those who are suffering today from the legacy of slavery are not only those in the former Caribbean colonies, where poverty and unemployment are rife, but the young people who form the third generation of migrants resident in British cities today — the young black British — all of whom suffer in some way from the legacy of slavery, most of whom suffer from various forms of social deprivation, and some of whom are actively involved in the gang life of British cities today.

Notes

[1] See chapter 7, The Zong Project, section 7.3.

[2] Acts of the Privy Council, London, 11 August 1596.

[3] *The Gentleman's Magazine*, Volume XXXIV, London, 1764, p. 492.

[4] Hansard, 12th May 1789.

[5] *Ibid*.

[6] Olaudah Equiano, *Equiano the African: Biography of a Self-Made Man*, University of Georgiana Press, Athens, Georgia, 2005, editor: Vincent Carretta, pp. 33–34.

[7] John Newton, quoted in Chris Hudson, *Son of Africa: The Story of Olaudah Equiano and The Campaign Against The Slave Trade*, SCM-Canterbury Press Ltd, Norwich, 2007, p. 8.

[8] See chapter 4, section 4.5.

[9] F O Syllon, *Black Slaves in Britain*, Oxford, 1974, p. 169.

[10] *Op. cit.*, p. 206.

[11] James Walvin, *Black Ivory – Slavery in the British Empire*, 2nd edition, Blackwell Publishing, Oxford, 2004, p. 19.

[12] Quoted in O Patterson, *The Sociology of Slavery*, London 1967, p. 163.

[13] Robin Blackburn, *The Overthrow of Colonial Slavery*, pp. 526, 528. quoted in Max B Ifill, *Slavery, Social Death or Communal Victory*, Economics and Business Research, Port of Spain, Trinidad, 1996, pp. 37–38.

Chapter Seven

THE ZONG PROJECT

Early in the year 2005, my wife and I were invited to join a national committee to make advance arrangements for the commemoration of the 200th anniversary of the Abolition of the Slave Trade in 2007. The committee was convened by the Ethnic Minorities Group of Churches Together in England. Our base was in Moggerhanger Park, Bedfordshire which was the eighteenth century home of the Thornton family, cousins of William Wilberforce and active abolitionists. We were planning an exhibition of 'Slavery Past and Present' as part of the 2007 commemorations, which was to include a model slave ship, but in the summer of 2006 it was decided to be more adventurous. We wanted to find a real replica eighteenth century slave ship and bring it into London, as no other group was known to be planning such a project. In order to facilitate this we set up a team to lead what became known as the 'Free at Last?' project, and we appealed to our supporters for financial support. There was a generous response which enabled the project to go ahead.

7.1 Finding a Replica Ship
In August 2006 we discovered that the square rigger used in the film *Amazing Grace* (in which it was named the *Madagascar*) was moored in Charlestown, St Austell, Cornwall. The owners were willing to lease it for the

period we required in March/April 2007. We went to see it in September and reached agreement on the alterations we would need to refit the ship as an eighteenth century slaver. We also negotiated with the Port of London Authority and Thames Luxury Cruisers for the use of Tower Pier and a mooring in the River Thames adjacent to Sugar Pier. We hired a 50-seater ferry to be available all day, with a constantly running service between the square rigger and Tower Pier.

7.2 The Royal Navy

We had earlier approached the Admiralty to explore the possibility of mooring alongside HMS Belfast. This was not possible but the Admiralty expressed considerable interest in the project and offered to provide a warship escort up the River Thames into the Pool of London. They said this would be part of the Navy's commemoration of their role in the abolition of the slave trade. They offered to lead the 'slave ship' into London as they would have done if they had captured the ship illegally running slaves after the passing of the Abolition of the Slave Trade Act in 1807. It was arranged that HMS Northumberland, a frigate, would join our slave ship at Greenwich where she was due to be re-fitted as a slaver. From there the frigate would lead the square rigger up the Thames, through Tower Bridge, to Sugar Pier, and HMS Northumberland would moor alongside HMS Belfast. Arrangements were also made for the Navy to send a contingent, including a naval chaplain and a Commodore, from Plymouth to Charlestown, Cornwall to take part in a commissioning ceremony of the ship for its mission to London.

A considerable amount of research, and consultation with both African and Caribbean leaders, was carried out in preparation for an exhibition of slavery on board the ship as part of its refit as an eighteenth century slaver. The exhibition was in three parts. The first was land based at All Hallows by the Tower; the second was on board the ship, and the third was in the church hall at All Hallows. The first part of the exhibition featured details of the Atlantic trade triangle, beginning with capture in Africa, transport across to the West Indies, sale in the slave market, followed by life on the sugar plantations.

7.3 The Slave Ship

The second part of the exhibition was on board the ship, where details of the sea crossing were realistically portrayed by sound and sight. Parties of up to 50 were escorted down Tower Hill to Tower Pier, accompanied by three of the 124 volunteers who served in this project. Each party boarded the specially hired 50-seater ferry for the short journey to where the slave ship was moored close to Sugar Pier (adjacent to the Tate and Lyle building). Following a short talk on the upper deck of the square rigger, each party went below to see and experience something of the conditions under which slaves were transported from West Africa to the Caribbean in the eighteenth century. Most members of the public found it a very moving experience, and those whose ancestors came from the Caribbean islands were often deeply affected. Down in the hold of the ship, in semi-darkness, there were the slatted shelves and chains on which the Africans were manacled in pairs. There was also a rolling presentation with sound track that brought sights and sounds of the Atlantic crossings.

The final part of the exhibition back in All Hallows presented details of the abolition campaign, featuring the main characters, both black and white, from the eight-eenth and early nineteenth centuries: William Wilberforce, Olaudah Equiano, Thomas Clarkson, Granville Sharp,

Hannah More, Henry Thornton and John Newton. It also focused on the legacy of slavery and some of the modern forms of slavery such as people trafficking, sex slavery and drugs that enslave people today.

7.4 Project Purpose

The primary purpose of the project was to expose a period of British history that has been hidden from sight for two hundred years. Bringing a slave ship into the Pool of London we believed would be the most dramatic means of communicating the reality and the monstrous cruelty, inhumanity and injustice of colonial slavery. But this was not conceived to be simply an educational project. It was designed to be a major step in *reconciliation* between white British people and people of African and African-Caribbean roots.

The ship was renamed the *Zong* for its visit to London as this was the most infamous of the eighteenth century slave trading vessels.[1] The ship, owned by two former Lord Mayors of Liverpool, sailed from the west coast of Africa in 1781, being licensed to carry 292 Africans. Captain Collingwood took on board 442 men, women and children, for whom there were insufficient provisions for a journey to the Caribbean that lasted almost three months and, as we have already recorded, he threw overboard 132 of them in an insurance scam.[2]

The *Zong* (2007) sailed through Tower Bridge with a mixed ethnic choir on deck singing 'Amazing Grace', escorted by HMS Northumberland that dropped anchor alongside HMS Belfast. There followed the official welcome and opening to the public of the exhibition on board the replica slave ship, which was performed by Mr Ken Livingstone, Mayor of London, on 29 March 2007. This attracted considerable interest from the media with wide coverage on television news and radio. It was the television news that brought the public in considerable numbers as there was no money in the £300,000 budget for advertising. The media coverage made a considerable impact upon many Londoners which brought them to see the ship and the Exhibition of Slavery Past and Present.

It was decided not to use the evenings on the slave ship for commercial purposes despite fears that we might not meet our budget. It did not seem right to have feasting and revelry on board a ship dedicated to commemorating the suffering of slaves. Instead, the evenings were used for seminars with invited speakers to stimulate discussion on subjects such as the 'Motivation of the Abolitionists', the 'Legacy of Slavery' and 'Slavery in the Modern World'.

Despite the lack of advertising, nearly 10,000 visitors came to visit the ship and to see the exhibition during the ten days the ship was open to the public. This was remarkable because many of them came through the recommendation of friends. Thus there was a steady increase in attendance throughout the time the ship was in London. The survey results revealed that 93% of those attending the exhibition said they would recommend to their friends that they attend.

Before the ship was opened to the public many people had expressed the view that people of West Indian origins would not wish to come to the ship because it would stir deep emotions which for them would be too painful. In fact the reverse proved to be true. Although there were fewer African and Caribbean visitors than Europeans on the first day, by the final weekend Caribbean people greatly outnumbered all others.

7.5 Painful Experience

The experience of going on board the *Zong,* and especially down into the cargo hold where slaves had been chained and manacled, was painful for many African-Caribbeans, knowing that this was how their forebears had been transported across the Atlantic. A coach party from Birmingham brought with them a large wreath which they placed in the slave pen on the lower deck. This simple action added to the pathos for many visitors, some of whom were in tears when they climbed back onto the upper deck.

Throughout the time the ship was in London there was a growing request for the ship to be a permanent feature in London so that the abolition of the slave trade could be suitably commemorated and future generations would be able to see something of a period in British history that has been neglected. At the suggestion of officers in the GLA, a petition was organised, calling for the ship to be permanently based in London. Although this was only available for the last few days, more than two thousand signatures were collected. There was such enthusiasm for the project to be permanently available in London that some visitors even took the forms to ask their friends to sign.

7.6 Caribbeans

The legacy of slavery was not only featured in the exhibition and in evening seminars but it was also frequently referred to in conversations with visitors. People of Caribbean origin have not forgotten that it was their fellow Africans who sold them to Europeans for transportation across the Atlantic. This knowledge adds to the socio/cultural differentials between Africans and Caribbeans that is to be seen in the different communities in Britain. People from the Caribbean islands have English names and are unable to trace their African origins by name, tribe or region. Conversations with visitors to the ship emphasised that it is not uncommon for West Indian young people to feel that the name they bear is still a form of branding that their forebears suffered on the plantations. Some of the Caribbean visitors were clearly angry that they still bore this legacy of slavery.

The survey revealed that although most people from the Caribbean had not been taught about slavery in school, they had significantly greater knowledge and interest in the subject than any other ethnic group. This was shown in the much higher proportion who had read books on slavery since leaving school. It was the older people from the Caribbean who found the experience most distressing, although their young people were more inclined to react with anger as they discovered the history of the slave trade. Almost all the Caribbean visitors to the *Zong* said they found the experience either 'sad' or 'distressing'. The party from Birmingham who placed a wreath of flowers in the slave pen said they were particularly thinking of the 1,300,000 Africans who lost their lives on the journey across the Atlantic, as well as their own forebears who were enslaved on the plantations in the Caribbean islands.

Some young people of African-Caribbean origins living in Peckham, south London came to visit the *Zong* because they saw it on the television news and were impressed with the multi-racial group of singers on board the ship as it sailed into London. They thought at first that this was a white man's attempts to whitewash the slave trade. But when they saw that the group of singers was black and white, young and old, they decided to come and see what it was all about. They said they had learned a lot because they were "never taught this stuff at school", and they wanted to know more about their roots.

The fact that this period of history had not been taught in school came out in conversation with hundreds of

Caribbeans. Among the comments of older people was that all the history they were taught in the West Indies was about English kings and queens. They were never taught about their own history. Many of them said that slavery is a subject that is never even talked about privately in their family groups because it was a taboo subject back home in the West Indies. Slavery was in the distant past, and older Caribbeans preferred to leave it there and not to discuss it. But among young people there is a real hunger to know their own history which they feel they have been denied for two hundred years.

7.7 Anger and Reconciliation

On arrival and seeing the first part of the exhibition there were reactions of anger among some African-Caribbeans. But all, except for one or two, changed their attitude by the time they had finished the two-hour experience of going around the exhibition and on board the ship and looking at the third part of the exhibition. Much of this anger had its source in the feeling that black people had been kept in ignorance of slavery as part of the white man's two hundred year conspiracy of silence. Only one man refused to pay the small fee of ten pounds for the conducted tour, on the grounds that his forebears had gone free — why should he pay to go on the ship? It was the objective of the project organisers that every visitor should be engaged in conversation by one of our staff or volunteers, so that any misunderstandings or emotional experiences could be dealt with in the context of reconciliation which was one of the main objectives of the whole project.

The success of this approach was underlined since, by the last few days of the ship being open to the public, the majority of those coming were of Caribbean origin. It was also a remarkable fact that, after being addressed by members of our staff who explained the purpose of the project, most of the Caribbeans applauded enthusiastically. After the visits to the ship, most of them went out of their way to express gratitude to our staff and volunteers for organising the project. Virtually all the Caribbean visitors signed the petition calling for the ship to be a permanent feature in London so that successive generations can learn the history of their origins.

Racism is endemic in British society and this forms part of the legacy of slavery. From the sixteenth to the eighteenth century there was an attitude in Britain that regarded African people as less than human. That attitude of superiority has never been eradicated. Although education and legislation can control behaviour, changing attitudes requires a process of reconciliation, because racism is usually unresponsive to rational processes.

7.8 Legacy of Slavery

There is not only a legacy of slavery in the white British population but also within the African community in Britain. Among many Africans there is a sense of superiority in respect of the African-Caribbeans. In a conversation between an African woman and Caribbean woman after both had been on board the *Zong*, the African was denying that there is any problem between them. The Caribbean woman said that she was married to an African man whose family had never accepted her. They always treated her badly and her African mother-in-law constantly referred to her as 'that slave woman'.

Teachers who visited the exhibition affirmed the difficulties of teaching the subject of slavery in a multi-racial context. They said that the Caribbean children found the subject particularly painful and embarrassing. The 200th anniversary of the abolition of the slave trade has, however, brought the subject of slavery into the curriculum of many schools, and it needs to be taught with care and sensitivity. This can most successfully be done within the context of reconciliation between the races.

The exhibition was not only designed to expose the cruelty of slavery and Britain's role in the slave trade but also the guilt of the church. Although there is evidence that church leaders such as John Wesley were vocal in opposition to slavery, many silently acquiesced, and at least one Church organisation employed slaves in Barbados. Records also show that the Bishop of Exeter received compensation for the emancipation of his slaves in 1833. On the positive side, the Christian faith of the abolitionists was also featured. It was their conviction that they had been called by God to stand against both Church and state in this campaign. This conviction enabled them to overcome the powerful vested interests of the rulers of the nation.

All this was featured in the exhibition, which led to many conversations with most visitors on the subject. During the visit of the *Zong* to London, among the 124 volunteers were several experienced historians, who were of great assistance to our staff team. This not only ensured that there was always an adequate staff/visitor ratio, but that we were able to deal with complex historical questions from visitors. Some of those who came were visitors to London from different parts of the world, and our broadly-based team of guides enabled us to engage most visitors in conversation and to deal with their questions.

As well as there always being an expert historian on hand, there were also trained counsellors available for those who found the experience on board the *Zong* to be distressing. All our staff and volunteers were not only familiar with the subject but were also committed to the concept of reconciliation. This was emphasised in conversations with visitors, in the free literature that was given to each visitor, and other papers that were available.

A series of evening seminars was organised, with invited guests on the upper deck of the *Zong* on subjects related to slavery past and present. These issues were addressed by some outstanding speakers who also formed a panel for questions and discussion. Seminar topics included 'The Legacy of Slavery' and 'Slavery Today'. They made a significant contribution to the whole event and opened up a number of avenues for creative social action.

7.9 Reconciliation

Reconciliation was also the focal point of a prayer time on Maundy Thursday evening, the traditional beginning of Easter, held on board the replica slave ship, where black and white leaders used the occasion to face up to the past and to wash one another's feet in the way that Jesus had washed his disciples' feet at the Last Supper before his crucifixion.

This theme of reconciliation was powerfully present in a Service of Commitment in All Hallows by the Tower when the *Zong* closed to the public on the final day of the exhibition. African, Caribbean and English church leaders committed themselves to work together in a programme of community action designed to overcome the legacy of slavery and to deal with the latent racism in all sections of British society. This act of commitment also included recognition of the various forms of modern slavery and a determination to seek ways of combating its scourge.

The willingness of almost all visitors to complete a survey, in which many people commented upon the high professional standard of the exhibition, underlined the success of the project and the need for greater public awareness of a hidden period of British colonial history.

7.10 Key Findings of the Survey[3]

1. Colonial slavery and the Atlantic slave trade have been largely unrecognised by the British public for the past 200 years. Only 9% of the white British population claimed to 'know a lot' about colonial slavery.

2. Older white British people have the least knowledge of Britain's involvement in the slave trade and colonial slavery.

3. Today's schoolchildren and teenagers have a significantly greater knowledge of colonial slavery and the slave trade than their parents and grandparents. 55% under 21 had been taught about slavery at school, compared with 37% of those aged 21 to 40.

4. Africans and Caribbeans in Britain have studied slavery and read books about the slave trade more than the white population – 66%, compared to only 43% of white British.

5. The experience of going on board the slave ship *Zong* and seeing the conditions suffered by enslaved Africans on the Atlantic slave trade was more emotionally disturbing for Africans and Caribbeans than for white British people. 57% of African visitors found the experience 'sad' or 'distressing', compared with 42% of white British.

6. There is a hunger among African-Caribbeans for exploring their roots by gaining a greater knowledge of the 18th century Atlantic slave trade and the life of their forebears in the Caribbean islands.

7. Many African-Caribbeans in Britain want to go back in history beyond the period of slavery to discover their African roots. The difficulty they experience in discovering their roots is part of what is slowly being recognised as the 'legacy of slavery'.

8. The 'legacy of slavery' today among African-Caribbeans is largely unrecognised by white British people.

9. White people in Britain today still carry attitudes of racial superiority that are part of the legacy of slavery.

Notes

[1] An historical account of the *Zong* is given in chapter 6, section 6.9.

[2] See details in chapter 6, section 6.9.

[3] The full report of the survey is available online on Issachar Ministries website.

Chapter Eight

WHITE SLAVERY: EIGHTEENTH AND NINETEENTH CENTURY BRITAIN

8.1 Age of Revolution

It was an age of revolution; political, social and technological. This was the background environment of the twenty year Parliamentary campaign to abolish the Atlantic slave trade. It was the late eighteenth and early nineteenth century, with Britain at war with France and America on the international scene, and struggling at home to avoid violent insurrection similar to the French Revolution. With the nation at war, there was a greater demand for home produced food but the Agricultural Revolution had provided landowners with mechanical equipment, and fewer labourers were required. Additionally, the enclosure of common land affected large numbers of small peasant farmers who were reduced to poverty, driving them to seek employment in the new urban industrial centres that were springing up around the country.

The enclosure of common land by powerful landowners was a grave injustice. It was a denial of rights to the poor which had been acknowledged for centuries. It left many poor families without the means of sustenance and stirred deep resentment of the workers against the upper classes as was expressed in an early eighteenth century ditty:

FREE AT LAST?

> They hang the man and flog the woman
> That steals a goose from off the common
> But leave the greater criminal loose
> That steals the common from the goose.[1]

Indeed, the Enclosure Acts marked the beginning of the great social class divide in Britain which has lasted until the present day. The rural peasants found themselves forced to migrate to the new industrial urban complexes where they formed a new class of landless urban poor. They were in a type of 'caste' situation from which there was no social mobility. Wilberforce was, therefore, sociologically accurate in describing this as a form of 'white slavery'.

The Industrial Revolution was greedy for labour but the houses provided by the new owners of industry were grossly inadequate, without running water or sanitation, creating ghettos of poverty and squalor overnight. For many, the new urban industrial world was far worse than they had endured in the countryside, where at least they had been able to grow food for themselves and they were usually cared for by the local squire in a feudal-like social situation. The new industrial entrepreneurs were not used to employing labour and they had no traditional social ties to their workers. They provided employment for which they fixed the rates of pay, and they provided accommodation for which they fixed the rents. But this created a situation in which the industrial workers were utterly dependent upon their employers and were powerless to improve their situation, which was described by contemporary radical journalists such as Cobbett and Hazlitt as worse than that of the black slaves in the West Indies.

8.2 White Slaves

William Cobbett was a fierce critic of Wilberforce, whom he described as a hypocrite who spent all his energies on behalf of the black slaves in the colonies, while ignoring the plight of the 'white slaves' on his own doorstep. Cobbett, however, had a vested interest as he was a journalist in the pay of the West India Group of Plantation Owners and he constantly depicted the African slaves as being well treated, well fed, and cared for by altruistic masters. He compared this with the cruelty and exploitation of workers in the cotton mills of Lancashire and the woollen mills of Yorkshire, and with the women and children who were sent down into the coal mines in England and Wales.

Cobbett was paid to oppose the abolition of the slave trade and his testimony regarding colonial slavery was unreliable, but he was certainly right in drawing attention to the appalling conditions in the factories and mines of Britain, and the unhealthy conditions in the burgeoning urban industrial areas. When the first national census was taken in 1801, the population of England was just under nine million. London was the only major city with a population of about half a million, the next largest being Bristol and Norwich, each with about 50,000. The towns were ramshackle warrens of squalor, dirt and disease. The streets were unpaved and narrow. There were no sanitary systems other than open cesspools in the courtyards of the rich. The houses of the poor were small, overcrowded, and often shared with their pigs and chickens.

Unemployment in the towns was high, with large numbers depending upon casual labour, with even the tradesmen, craftsmen and artisans working long hours for modest wages that barely raised their wives and children above subsistence level. It is small wonder that in these circumstances, crime was widespread and violence was a major characteristic of society. Children were routinely abused and cruelly treated. Domestic service in the homes of the rich was drudgery with long hours of hard physical work. Exploitation and unhealthy living conditions were the norm. Hogarth's pictures of London life show the lean and hungry faces of the poor and depict something of the bitterness of despair that characterised life in this period.[2]

8.3 Combination Acts

During the eighteenth century, many workers in different industries and occupations formed Friendly Societies and trade clubs, often meeting in local taverns or inns. Their objective was mutual support and seeking the ability to protect members' jobs, to raise pay levels and to improve working conditions. They were, in fact, early forms of trades unions, but they were resisted by employers. In 1799 and 1800 the Government introduced measures to restrict the power of workers to act together. The Combination Act 1800 made it punishable by prison sentences for workers to:

- Attend strike meetings;
- Combine with others to force employers to raise wages;
- Combine to force employers to improve working conditions;
- Engage in picketing;
- Help to finance strikes.

During the first half of the nineteenth century there were many disturbances and serious riots. Memories of the French Revolution were still fresh in the minds of the ruling classes, who feared for their lives if the riots should get out of hand and lead to revolution. The Radicals were not sufficiently organised to turn a riot into a revolution. They were simply desperate people, driven by poverty to protest about low wages such as in the Luddite riots of 1811 and 1812 involving Nottingham weavers, and the mill workers of Lancashire and Yorkshire, where men were killed. It was the inability to feed their families that drove the poor to riot when the price of basic foods such as bread were increased through the Corn Law of 1815 which banned the import of cheap corn in order to protect the income of landowners. The riots in London following the Corn Law, and the Spa Fields riot of 1816, were enough to cause the authorities serious concern, although nothing was actually done to relieve the social conditions of the poor.

Further riots took place in Nottingham and Manchester in 1817, and the latter led up to the huge peaceful demonstration in St Peter's Fields, Manchester in 1819, where the magistrates allegedly read the Riot Act and the crowd had not dispersed after the statutory one hour period. This had tragic consequences when soldiers on horseback rode through the crowd, swinging their cutlasses. The so-called 'Peterloo Massacre' shocked the country but still there were no moves by the Government to relieve the suffering of the poor. It was always the rights of the ruling classes that were upheld.

The Poor Law Amendment Act 1834 was intended to change the Poor Laws that had been operating since 1601 with the parish system of providing local help for those in need. In fact, it cut aid to able-bodied workers and forced the unemployed into a new form of workhouse which broke up families, providing separate accommodation for:

- The aged and impotent
- Mothers and children
- Able-bodied females
- Able-bodied males.

There was widespread criticism of the whole system of poor relief which had the effect of spreading pauperism rather than eradicating it. Thomas Arnold, in an 1832 newspaper article, said that the whole system operated 'under the mask of kindness to the poor' but was really 'one of the most degrading systems of oppression'.[3] *The Christian Record*, a newspaper published from 1828 under the direction of Alexander Haldane, with its own brand of Protestantism, declared the system to be 'vicious in principle and intolerant in practice'.[4] The 1834 Act, more than any other, aroused a persistent, burning sense of injustice among the working classes. Webb takes the view that Poor Law policy in this period was largely based upon the Malthusian view of the dangers of overpopulation.[5] But Poor Law policy in England remained basically unchanged until 1909, when a Royal Commission appointed by Balfour four years earlier presented its report.

8.4 Children Exploited

Children were the most vulnerable victims of industrialisation. They were routinely beaten and cruelly treated, working long hours in appalling conditions. Children began work at an early age, providing an instant source of cheap labour. They were employed in the mills and factories as well as being sent down the mines to work long hours in unhealthy and dangerous conditions. Many of these children were orphans who had been brought up in institutions and handed over to unscrupulous employers as apprentices, which was a form of indentured labour not unlike that which was practised in some of the West Indian colonies, notably Guyana, where large numbers of Indian workers were indentured.

The first sign of social conscience in regard to the exploitation of children was seen in regard to boys being sent up chimneys as chimney sweeps. Many of these boys suffered appalling injuries through falling, and had serious burns to their feet as they were forced to walk barefoot on burning coals. It took more than twenty years of campaigning before an Act of Parliament was passed in 1788 to curb these excesses of cruelty to children. William Wilberforce and Henry Thornton, and the Clapham Group of which they were leaders, played a prominent part in this campaign. They also pressed for a limit to the number of hours that children could work in any one day, but it took many more years before this was achieved.

The issue of child labour was brought before Parliament in the debate leading up to the First Factory Act of 1802, although Thomas Gisborne had been the first to raise the issue in 1794, calling for legislation to provide relief for children working in factories. It was Sir Robert Peel (the Elder) who put it into the Bill in 1802, but it was rejected. In fact it took another 44 years before the British Parliament finally decided that it was not right for children to be forced to work more than ten hours a day in factories and mills and down the mines. The scandal of child slavery in Britain was a stain on the nation that has left a permanent scar upon industrial relationships between workers and management. It has had a lasting effect upon social class attitudes which persist today and is part of the legacy of white slavery in Britain which goes right back to the Enclosures Act and the early days of the Industrial Revolution.

8.5 Yorkshire Slavery

The issue of child labour dropped out of public attention for a number of years when the war with France overshadowed Home Affairs, but it was revived twenty-two years later in 1824 by The Rev. George Bull, a Yorkshire clergyman, speaking at a conference of Sunday School workers in Hull. He drew attention to the difficulty of teaching children who were working long hours in unhealthy conditions. There was no state education—churches and voluntary groups provided the only available education for the poor. Michael

Thomas Sadler, who was a Member of Parliament, took the campaign into the House of Commons, where he pleaded for the abolition of what he called 'Yorkshire slavery', but it was another eight years before the House voted on the subject, and even then the legislation was not sufficiently watertight to ban child labour in the factory system. By now, at least, the issue had been brought to the attention of the whole nation.

The campaign aimed at reducing the working hours of children to ten hours each day. Children as young as nine years of age were routinely employed in factories from 6.00 a.m. to 7.00 p.m. In some factories they were employed for even longer hours and were at the mercy of cruel and brutal overseers who subjected them to both physical and sexual abuse. Bull made close enquiries of his Sunday School children and discovered that the situation was even worse than he feared, and he reported on, 'The appalling mischief to health, social order, morality and religion, which are inseparable from the ordinary system of nearly 14 hours a day.'[6]

8.6 First Bill Presented

There were strong similarities between the battle to abolish the African slave trade and the battle to abolish the slavery inflicted upon white children in Britain. Thirty years after the First Factory Act had brought the plight of children to the attention of Parliament, the matter again came before the House of Commons. It was in 1832 that Sadler introduced a Bill to reduce the length of children's work to ten hours per day but it was vehemently opposed by the Government who did everything possible to discredit the evidence presented by Sadler. Many Members of Parliament were wealthy industrialists or had shares in industries from which they profited from the cheap labour provided by children. Their fears of the effects upon the economy were similar to the arguments brought against Wilberforce by those who feared that the abolition of the colonial slave trade would be disastrous for the economy. As a diversionary tactic the Government set up a Select Committee to investigate. Even *The Times* thought this was outrageous:

> Why a Select Committee should be required to ascertain whether it be right and proper to confine infants of seven, eight, nine, or 10 years of age to more than 12 hours a day at unremitting labour in the atmosphere of a factory is beyond our imagination.[7]

A year later the Select Committee was replaced by a Royal Commission which was widely seen as yet another delaying tactic and there were many public protests around the country. Archbishop Howley spoke in the House of Lords in support of Sadler's Bill saying that the present system was injurious to the health of children. He said that it was:

> "A disgrace in a Christian and civilised country to allow such a system to continue, merely for the sake of putting money into the pockets of the master manufacturers."[8]

But the Bill was rejected. The manufacturers were strongly represented in Parliament and there were few to plead the cause of the workers.

8.7 Factory Conditions

Conditions in the factories were appalling, with unguarded machines making accidents commonplace. Children were regularly beaten by cruel overseers and infants were employed to do dangerous jobs such as crawling under machines when there was a breakdown. A report from the Children's Employment Commissioners in 1843 said:

In Willenhall the children are shamefully and most cruelly beaten with a horsewhip, strap, stick, hammer, handle, file, or whatever tool is nearest to hand, or are struck with the clenched fist or kicked.[9]

In a further report about lace making in Nottingham it stated:

If the statement of a mother be correct, one of her children, four years of age, works 12 hours a day with only an interval of a quarter of an hour for each meal at breakfast, dinner and tea, and never going out to play: and two more of her children, one six and the other eight years of age, work in summer from 6.00 am, till dusk, and in winter from seven in the morning till 10 at night, 15 hours a day.[10]

In a Parliamentary debate leading to the Factory Act of 1833, Sadler again tried to reduce the number of hours children could work in all factories to ten each day, but this too was unsuccessful. Outside Parliament, Richard Oastler drew attention to 'Yorkshire slavery' in the mills of Bradford. In an 1832 speech he said:

'I have never ceased to use every legal means, for the purpose of emancipating these innocent slaves. On one occasion I was in the company of a West India slave master and three Bradford spinners; the spinners were obliged to be silent when the slave–owner said, "Well, I have always thought myself disgraced by being the owner of black slaves, but we never, in the West Indies, thought it was possible for any human being to be so cruel as to require a child of nine years old to work 12 hours a day; and that, you acknowledge, is your regular practice."'[11]

Richard Oastler had begun his leadership of the '10 Hour Campaign' in 1830 when he visited a wealthy industrialist, whom he found reading the Bible and was deeply troubled in his conscience by what he described as "The cruelties which are practised in our mills." On that same day, 29 September 1830, Oastler wrote his famous 'Yorkshire slavery' letter in which he compared the mills of Yorkshire with the plantations on which African slaves were employed:

> Thousands of our fellow creatures… are at this very moment existing in a state of slavery *more horrid* than are the victims of that hellish system, *'colonial slavery'*.[12]

The 1833 Factory Act did prohibit the employment of children under nine years of age in textile mills. Most importantly it appointed Government inspectors to carry out regular inspections of the factories to ensure that the law was observed, but in fact the law was never uniformly enforced. Children were still employed in the mines, mills and factories of Britain. In 1842 a Coalmines Act was passed in the face of huge opposition from the mine owners who regularly used children in deep mines where the head room was so low that men could not work. The new law banned the employment underground of boys less than ten years of age and all women and girls irrespective of age. An inspector of mines was also appointed, but once again the law was not enforced and many mine owners continued to use women and children. In a speech in Parliament in 1842, Lord Ashley (later Shaftesbury) reported that in some mines:

> "The underground ways are so low only little boys can work in them, which they do naked, and often in mud and water, dragging sledge tubs by the girdle and chains." He said that in Halifax "girls from five years old regularly perform the same work as boys." [13]

8.8 Ten Hour Act

It was not until 1847 that 'The 10 Hour Act' was finally passed through Parliament, limiting the number of hours children could be employed to ten hours a day, and the means of inspection were set up to ensure that the will of Parliament was carried out. This was *forty-five years* from the time the plight of children was first brought before the British Parliament!

It seems incredible to us in the twenty-first century that a British Parliament should have taken so long to recognise the cruelty and unacceptability of forcing children as young as six to work long hours in dangerous places and given no education, with no prospects of escaping the poverty into which they were born. It is an illustration of the gross inequality of the parliamentary system that denied the vote to ordinary working men, who had no representation in the government of the land and were powerless to resist the will of the ruling classes. Even the 1832 Reform Act did not extend the franchise to all people. In fact, the actual number of people who voted in a General Election in the UK did not increase until after the 1867 Reform Act. The property qualification excluded most men in the population, and all women were excluded. In fact, it was not until 1928, almost one hundred years after the first Reform Act, that all citizens in Britain were given the vote regardless of age, gender or wealth.

There can be no doubt that this long battle to release children from what was widely accepted as a situation of slavery in Britain, and to accept the justice of giving the vote to all citizens of the land, was formative in creating social class attitudes in the whole of the UK. The older generation today are the children of the generation that suffered the loss of one million men in the First World War that was believed to be the war to end all wars and to create a 'nation fit for heroes'. The disillusionment of the interwar years, of poverty, unemployment and the struggle for social justice, confirmed the experience of the Victorian working classes that the holders of wealth and power would not willingly surrender their positions of social privilege. The general strike of 1929, and the long marches of the unemployed from the North, had the effect of institutionalising social class differentials and attitudes between workers in the North and those in what was perceived to be more privileged positions in the South — attitudes which were institutionalised over a period of two centuries from the early days of the Industrial Revolution and still remain today.

8.9 Masters and Slaves Mentality

The first half of the nineteenth century was a time of considerable social unrest which was exacerbated by the Poor Law Amendment Act 1834. This was seen as a direct attack upon working people. It effectively abolished parish aid and forced the unemployed poor into newly established workhouses where families were broken up, with men in separate units from the women and children. The Act created deep resentment among the poor, not only among the unemployed but among all working people. It not only increased the sense of alienation from industry, noted by Karl Marx,[14] which had been growing since the Industrial Revolution, but it greatly increased the social distance between the ruling classes and workers. It further institutionalised the 'masters and slaves' mentality that was to affect industrial relations in Britain for decades to come.

Hopes of moving towards a more representative form of government were strong in the public debate leading up to the 1832 Reform Act, but there was considerable disappointment at the limitations of the Act. In the widespread anger that followed, a small group of social reformers led by William

Lovett, Secretary of the London Working Men's Association, and John Roebuck, a radical Member of Parliament, drew up a 'People's Charter' in 1838 with six points. They were:

- A vote for every adult male over 21;
- A secret ballot;
- Annual Parliaments;
- No property qualification for MPs;
- Payment of a salary for MPs;
- Constituencies of equal size.

8.10 Chartist Movement

This triggered what became known as the 'Chartist Movement', which prefigured the trades union movement, although its objectives were more political than related to labour and employment conditions. Chartism was gaining support among the working classes in the wake of the suppression of 'combinations', or meetings of workers to discuss wages and conditions of work. The cruel treatment of the Tolpuddle Martyrs in 1834, who were deported to Australia, caused widespread resentment. They were workers from the mining village of Tolpuddle in Dorset who had tried to hold discussions with their employers after their miserably low wages had been cut from nine shillings to six shillings a week. They were convicted of administering an unlawful oath under the Mutiny Act of 1749 which had only been intended for marine offences. Their conviction provoked large-scale demonstrations in London and other cities. Further unrest among workers followed the passing of the Poor Law Amendment Act the same year (1834). In May 1842 a petition was organised with over three million signatures calling for the 'People's Charter' to be recognised by Parliament. It was summarily rejected, which provoked nationwide anger. A report in the *North Star* commented:

Three and a half millions have quietly, orderly, soberly, peaceably but firmly asked of their rulers to do justice; and their rulers have turned a deaf ear to that protest. Three and a half millions of people have asked permission to detail their wrongs, and enforce their claims for RIGHT, and the 'House' has resolved they should not be heard! Three and a half millions of the slave class have held out the olive branch of peace to the enfranchised and privileged classes and sought for a firm and compact union, on the principle of EQUALITY BEFORE THE LAW; and the enfranchised and privileged have refused to enter into a treaty! The same class is to be a slave class still. The mark and brand of inferiority is not to be removed. The assumption of inferiority is still to be maintained. The people are not to be free.[15]

8.11 Violent Disorders

Public unrest grew in face of the refusal of Parliament to listen to the grievances of the people. Throughout 1842 and 1843 there was a wave of strikes and demonstrations which alarmed the authorities and increased fears of a French-style insurrection. Three petitions were presented to Parliament — in 1839, 1842 and 1848 — but there was no positive response from Government. In many places, particularly in the textile areas of Yorkshire and Lancashire, there were violent disorders, sometimes with armed suppression, arrests and deportations. In Stoke-on-Trent three of the Chartists were shot dead while rioters burned the Town Hall and other public buildings. In some areas demonstrators disabled factory machinery in protest against the loss of jobs through the advent of more advanced mechanisation.

Although wages slowly rose during the 1850s and 1860s and most working people were better fed, there was still unrest about social and working conditions and the unwillingness of Parliament to surrender the monopoly of power enjoyed by the upper classes and the wealthy owners of industry. Riots and demonstrations undoubtedly played a part in persuading Disraeli, in the 1867 Reform Act, to give the vote to all male householders living in urban areas. The qualification was that they had to be men over 21 and either a householder or lodger paying at least ten pounds a year in rent. So there was still a property condition to having a vote in the affairs of the nation, and rural workers were excluded. The workers who had been campaigning for more than forty years saw this small concession, grudgingly conceded by the landowners and masters of industry, as almost derisory. It only served to confirm the class warfare which was inherent in the industrialised feudal system that had already become institutionalised in British society.

8.12 Trade Unions Emerge

The Chartist Movement eventually gave way to the New Model Trades Unions which began emerging in the 1850s, and their legality was confirmed by the provisions of the Friendly Societies Act of 1855. But the introduction of Trade Unions, with their paid officials and central organisation, by no means eradicated industrial unrest or disputes between masters and workers. It did, however, give power to the workers' organisations to negotiate with their employers on behalf of the workers. But the die was already cast, not only for industrial relations, but also for social class relationships across the nation.

Just as in the West Indies and the Americas the African slaves were essential for the rapid economic growth of colonial prosperity, so too were the white slaves of the Industrial Revolution in Britain. Britain could not have become the workshop of the world at the hub of a prosperous international commercial trade network, presided over by the mightiest empire in world history, without the cheap labour supplied by its forced-labouring black slaves in the Caribbean and its white slaves in Britain. Just as at the end of the eighteenth century more than three-quarters of the British economy was linked with colonial slavery, an even greater percentage of her manufacturing wealth for most of the nineteenth century was dependent upon 'white slavery'.

8.13 Miners' Strike

The long struggle for Parliamentary representation and for the emancipation of the working classes from the disenfranchised masses left its mark upon both industrial relationships and community relations. These attitudes of class warfare lasted well into the second half of the twentieth century and soured relationships in industry that were particularly seen in the strikes of the 1970s. The 'us and them' attitude towards industrial disputes was also clearly in evidence in the 1980s in the bitter dispute with the miners led by Arthur Scargill during Margaret Thatcher's premiership. In 2009, on the 25th anniversary of the 1984 strike, *The Guardian* published an article by Arthur Scargill setting out his version of events:

> At that time, Britain's coal industry was the most efficient and technologically advanced in the world, a result of a tripartite agreement, the 'Plan for Coal', signed by a Labour Government, the National Coal Board (NCB) and the mining trade unions in 1974, and endorsed by Thatcher in 1981. And yet, shortly after I became National President of the NUM in 1982 I was sent anonymously a copy of a secret plan prepared by NCB chiefs earmarking 95 pits for closure, with the loss of 100,000 miners' jobs. This plan had been prepared on Government instructions following the miners' successful unofficial strike in 1981.[16]

Scargill lays the blame for the failure of the 1984 strike firmly in the hands of Mrs Thatcher. He says that the National Coal Board, under pressure from the Prime Minister, had agreed to a phased closure of coal pits in different areas. The miners' strike and picketing of power stations, starving them of fuel for the generation of electricity, brought them to the edge of victory, but the Government managed to break the strike by persuading some of the miners' leaders to go against their union. There is little doubt that Mrs Thatcher's motives, both for provoking the miners' strike and for breaking it, were aimed at curbing the power of the unions. This was all part of the ongoing war between workers and rulers in Britain which began back in the time of the eighteenth century Industrial Revolution.

8.14 Class War

That class war is still very much alive in Britain today. It affects community relationships at all levels in society and it is even to be seen in the way British people judge each other by their accent and language. It is highly influential in the voting pattern of the population, especially those of the older generation. The 'white slavery', identified in the eighteenth and nineteenth centuries, is still present today in attitudes, although not in reality. It is to be seen in the underlying resentment of many working people towards the wealth enjoyed by the ruling classes. This has been much exacerbated since 2007–8 by the revelations of greed and corruption in financial institutions and the much publicised excessive bonuses paid to traders and executives in the banks. Social class tensions are also discernible in the treatment of workers by employers and in the manner of professionals towards those who are in 'inferior' positions in society.

8.15 'Plebgate'

A much publicised example was seen in what became known as the 'Plebgate' incident in Downing Street on 19 September 2012 when a Cabinet Minister, Andrew Mitchell, the Government Chief Whip, was refused permission to cycle out of the main gates and directed to walk through the passenger gate. Mitchell admitted that he had sworn at the police officer but strongly denied using the word 'pleb' in his confrontation. The Police Federation, who were in dispute with the Government over cuts to their pensions, used this to politicise the incident. Newspaper photographs appeared showing policemen wearing clothing with the words, 'PC Pleb and Proud'. According to a report in *The Times*, 'The Police Federation crammed the airwaves, waved banners outside the Tory party conference in Birmingham and eventually got their man' — the Chief Whip was forced to resign.[17]

Three months later an investigative journalist discovered that an email supposedly sent by a member of the public claiming to have witnessed the Downing Street incident was, in fact, sent by a serving police officer who was not even present. The email had confirmed the record in the police log claiming that the Chief Whip had used the word 'pleb' in abuse of the officer and this was crucial in leading to his resignation, although he continued to deny using the word. It was only at this point that CCTV footage showing that there were no members of the public present at the time of the incident was made available to Mr Mitchell or to Number 10, although this should have been made available on day one. This caused the re-opening of the whole incident and calls for Andrew Mitchell to be reinstated in his job, although it took a year before the Independent Police Authority reported on the incident and even longer before the Police Officer claiming to have witnessed the incident admitted in court that he had lied.

The significance of this event is not simply the politicising of the police who, traditionally, have maintained political neutrality since their foundation. The incident was of great significance in terms of the ongoing social class warfare that has characterised British society since the early days of the Industrial Revolution nearly three hundred years ago. David Cameron, as Prime Minister and leader of the Conservative Party, had been striving to expunge the old Tory image of class superiority from his party. The allegation, although unproven, that one of his ministers had used a term of social class abuse to a police officer was politically damaging. Its significance was that it confirmed working class suspicions that nothing had really changed in the political ruling class.

8.16 Social Class Attitudes

These attitudes of superiority/inferiority that are institution-alised in British society inevitably have the greatest effect upon those who live in an environment where social mobility is extremely rare. Young people living in inner-city areas where they lack the opportunities to move into higher education, which would open doors of occupational and economic advancement for them, experience the greatest frustration. With all normal routes to social mobility blocked, the only way they can achieve the possession of wealth that is deemed highly desirable in a materialistic, advertising driven, acquisitive society is through 'criminal' activity.

The attitudes in our present-day social class system have strong elements of the legacy of slavery deriving from roots in both the former colonial system and in industrial exploitation. Young people in inner-city areas feel they have no opportunity to share in the wealth of the nation and they are powerless to change the system that determines their life chances. We are, today, reaping the harvest of injustice sown by former generations. The effects of these institutionalised social systems are extremely difficult to eradicate, and their associated attitudes are only responsive to radical changes of mindset, which in turn are dependent upon actual social change.

In my long experience of living and working in the communities of inner-city areas of London, it seems clear to me that it is the mindset associated with the legacy of slavery (black and white) that is at the root of the social issues that led to the Tottenham riots in August 2011 which spread to other similar areas of social deprivation. Unless the root causes of these social issues and their links with the legacy of slavery are recognised and faced by society, the day will come when we will see a repeat of the Tottenham riots in our inner-city areas. In times of economic austerity that day may be sooner than we expect.

Notes

[1] Asa Briggs, *A Social History of England,* Book Club Associates, London, 1983, p. 174.

[2] Clifford Hill, *The Wilberforce Connection*, Monarch books, Oxford, 2004, p. 76.

[3] Thomas Arnold, *Thirteen Letters on our Social Condition* published in *The Sheffield Courant*, Sheffield, 1832, quoted in Herbert Schlossberg, *The Silent Revolution and The Making of Victorian England*, Ohio State University Press, Columbus, 2000, p. 162.

[4] *The Record,* 22 March 1838.

[5] R K Webb, *Modern England – From the 18th Century to the Present*, George Allen and Unwin Ltd, London, 1969, p. 243.

[6] J V C Gill, *The Ten Hours Parson*, SPCK, London, 1959, p. 19.

[7] *The Times*, 17 March 1832.

[8] Reported in *The Times* 2 March 1832.

[9] Quoted in Philip Sauvain, *British Economic and Social History*, Stanley Thornes Ltd, Cheltenham, 1987, p. 277.

[10] *Ibid.*, p. 277.

[11] Quoted in Philip Sauvain, *British Economic and Social History 1700–1817,* Stanley Thornes Ltd, Cheltenham, 1987, p. 279.

[12] J T Ward, *The Factory Movement 1830–55*, London, McMillan, 1962, p. 34. Quoted in Schlossberg, *op. cit.*, p. 271.

[13] Quoted in Sauvain, *op. cit.*, p. 282.

[14] Karl Marx, in his *Economic and Philosophic Manuscripts 1844,* noted 'Alienation' (*Entfremdung*) as the systemic result of living in a socially stratified society. He said that social class alienates a person from his or her humanity because under the capitalist mode of production the worker loses the ability of self-determination and any right to benefit from the goods and services produced by his own labour.

[15] *The Northern Star and National Trades Journal*, Vol. X, No. 458, London, 1846.

[16] *The Guardian*, 7 March 2009.

[17] *The Times,* 20 December 2012.

Chapter Nine

FAMILY AND CULTURE (PART 1)

No analysis of the social situation underlying the riots would be complete without considering the family and cultural background of those involved. In this chapter we will look at two aspects of the socio-historical background, and in the next we will look at the family in Britain from the 1950s. The two issues examined in this chapter are: family life in Jamaica in the 1950s and 1960s, and family life among first generation West Indian migrants in the UK.

A report by the Fatherhood Institute published in March 2010 showed that black fathers in Britain today are twice as likely as white British fathers to live apart from their children. They found similarly high rates of non-resident fatherhood among children of mixed race heritage, and the report stated that the main reasons for non-resident fatherhood in both the black and mixed heritage families are the same as those found among white fathers: low socio-economic status, unemployment, low standard of education. It further identified an additional factor as that of the experience of racism and institutionalised racism.

The report also noted that where children are raised in a family where the father is absent this does not necessarily mean that they had no contact with the father. It said that 'visitation fatherhood' in black Caribbean communities is common in the UK, but it has its origins not among the first generation of immigrants in the 1950s and 60s, but it is a practice that has been commonly acceptable in the West Indies since the early days of emancipation in the 1830s. This statement is highly significant and requires elaboration. It is not just fatherhood, but the whole pattern of family life among West Indian immigrants and Black British Caribbean families in the UK which has its origins in the West Indian islands where traditions were established during the period of colonial slavery that have persisted until the present day. We will look first at family life in Jamaica which was the culture brought to the UK by the first generation of migrants.

9.1 Family Life in Jamaica – Household Types

In the 1940s and 1950s, family life in Jamaica was differentiated by social researchers in four types of household. T S Simey[1] distinguished the four principal family types to be found in West Indian society as: (A) 'Christian families', which he defined as 'patriarchal units based on legal marriage'; (B) 'faithful concubinage', also patriarchal but without legal sanction; (C) 'companionate unions' or 'consensual habitation' of less than three years' duration; (D) 'disintegrate families', consisting of women with their children or grandchildren.

Henriques identified a similar typology although he changed (C) to 'maternal, or grandmother family' and (D) to 'keeper family'.[2] Both of these studies were carried out in the 1940s; then, in the 1950s, two more studies were carried out by R T Smith[3] and Edith Clarke,[4] both of which had a firmer sociological basis. There were strong similarities in each of the four studies, although Smith did not distinguish between legal marriage and common law unions which he said were sociologically identical. The weakness of Smith's analysis was that he failed to take account of the accepted social differentiation among lower class sections of the population where marriage had considerable significance as a predicator of social status. Marriage denoted a higher status in society which people in both working class and middle class groups sought to achieve; hence its sociological significance which biases results if ignored.

Both Simey and Henriques distinguished between stable and unstable conceptual cohabitations on the one hand and 'Christian marriage' on the other, primarily by reference to differences of economic situation, whereas Clarke noted the differences in mating relationships. It is to these mating practices that we need to look in order to understand the formation of both the maternal and the 'keeper family' households.

The household that is headed by a grandmother without the support of a man often originates through a girl becoming pregnant while still living at home. If the father of the child is working and able to contribute to household expenses he is often welcomed to come to live with the girl, but this is not usually the case. So the girl remains in her mother's household and her mother looks after the baby while the girl completes her schooling or seeks employment. Sometimes this means leaving home, in which case the grandmother brings up the child as her own and the girl sends money back for the support of the child. If, at a later time, the girl moves in with a man who is willing to support her, she will send for the child. If this new relationship produces other children they might either keep the 'outside child' or send him back to the grandmother or some other relative.

This new relationship would come under the heading of a 'keeper family' in which the couple agreed to live together in a temporary union. They each continue working and contributing to the household budget, but if the union continues over a number of years it would come under the heading of faithful concubinage. If the union produces a number of children its continuation may be determined by economic factors. Sometimes the man feels the pressures upon him too great and he simply goes away, leaving the woman alone. She may struggle on as a single mother or she may return to her family home and come under the shelter of her mother. This would be particularly typical of a household where there is a small amount of land for subsistence farming and the extra hand would be welcomed by the grandmother. But if the man had regular employment the couple may well decide to stay together and in due course they may marry.

9.2 Marriage

Although, as noted in Chapter 2, slavery is rarely discussed, even privately, among Jamaicans, many of their social customs originated in that period. This is particularly true for marriage and the structures of family life. There was a time when marriage was actually illegal for slaves under colonial law. At that time it was only the white section of the population who married with a church ceremony and a feast provided for all the 'county' folk. This established the pattern of marriage as the ideal, but it was not for the poor. Over time this practice was gradually extended to the fair coloured part of the population as the colour code dominated social class system emerged. This happened particularly after the emancipation, when planters who had established a relationship with a favourite slave woman felt free to marry her. The children, particularly if they had very fair skin, formed a new social class that influenced the development of the whole class system in the West Indies.

The new upper classes were careful to instruct their children in strict rules regarding sexual relationships to ensure that they maintained monogamous family structures.

The girls in particular would be carefully guarded although the boys were allowed to sow their wild oats provided they did not marry outside their white or fair skin equals. Social mobility for a black man was rare although it could be achieved through economic advancement. If a black man managed to acquire wealth it was socially acceptable for him to marry someone of a lighter skin which would gain him acceptance into the highest social class. Both working class and middle class men would seek to choose a partner of fair skin and with European shape features, but if they were to be accepted by the upper classes it was essential that they should marry rather than live in a common law union.

It was not only the upper classes who valued marriage. In the 1950s and 1960s, at the time of the large-scale emigration to the UK, the custom in family life in the working classes was to form various types of consensual relationships as noted above. If such a relationship of faithful concubinage became long term, it would usually lead to marriage when the couple reached mature years and they could afford to marry in the appropriate style, which, as we have observed, meant not only providing the appropriate clothes but also paying for food and drink and a celebration for the whole village or local community.

Marriage in the Caribbean traditionally represents a new status in society so that even the working class woman would expect her husband to be responsible for her and she would not expect to have to go out to work. Ideally she would expect to have a maid to do the housework, leaving her free to exercise her new status in the community. Many middle class families employ a school leaver to whom they pay a tiny weekly wage and provide basic accommodation. This contrasts with a concubine relationship where the woman is responsible for her own maintenance and is wholly responsible for the children. In marriage the man accepts responsibility for the woman and there is a shared responsibility for children.

A further difference between marriage and common law unions is seen in terms of authority within the household. In what Henriques termed 'Christian marriage' the family becomes a patriarchal unit. The husband assumes overall authority within the family and his word is law. This is one reason why many women prefer to stay in a common law union because they know that they will sacrifice their personal freedom. It was not unusual for husbands to beat their wives if they were displeased with them. In families where the man was in control, the children were often severely punished for wrongdoing. In all types of family physical punishment of children was common in the 1950s and 1960s. It was common for mothers to do a great deal of shouting as well as beating disobedient children, but it was the fathers who were most severe.

9.3 Sexual Relationships and 'Promiscuity'

Edith Clarke, in her 1957 study of working class communities in Jamaica, noted that:

> Not only is sexual activity regarded as natural; it is unnatural not to have a child and no woman who has not proved that she can bear one is likely to find a man to be responsible for her since no man is going to propose marriage to such a woman.... Just as a woman is only considered really a woman after she has borne a child, so the proof of a man's maleness is the impregnation of a woman. There is, therefore, no incentive for either men or women to avoid parenthood even in promiscuous relationships; on the contrary, it is the hallmark of adulthood and normal, healthy living.[5]

It was common practice in the 1960s in Jamaica for mothers, as their daughters approached adolescence, to give stern warnings against engaging in casual sexual relationships, although no such warnings were usually given to boys who were expected to engage in sexual experimentation if the opportunity arose. All social classes in Jamaica smiled with benign tolerance upon such male activities. Sexual experimentation began at quite an early age in working class communities, especially in rural environments where children played together on the way home from school. If the daughter had a steady friendship with a young man and there was every possibility that this might develop into a lasting relationship, the mother might encourage the boy to come and stay in her house where she could have some influence upon the relationship. But long-term relationships between working class black young men and girls were rare.

Such relationships were more likely to occur after a girl had had her first pregnancy and met with an older man who was prepared to enter into a permanent relationship. In such a case it was not uncommon for them to build a dwelling on the girl's mother's land and set up home together. The mother would welcome having a man on the property provided he was willing to engage in practical tasks. If the relationship did not last, the man would have no rights to the property: he would leave and the girl would stay, and her children would have rights of inheritance. If the land was too small to maintain a large family, the boys would be encouraged to leave when they were old enough and inheritance would go to one of the girls.

The mother or grandmother was always the central figure in a child's life but fathers were often an enigma. This was largely due to the high rate of illegitimacy which Edith Clarke notes: 'was directly related to sexual promiscuity, parental irresponsibility and the looseness of conjugal ties.'[6] But defining 'legitimacy' and 'illegitimacy' in the context of working class West Indian family life has always been notoriously difficult. In the 1960s the illegitimacy rate, that is those children who were registered at birth as being born outside a legal marriage, averaged 71%. But many of these children would have been raised in families of faithful concubinage, although Henriques estimated that this group was no more than 20% or 25% of the total population. So, if he is right, roughly half the population of children in Jamaica would have been raised in families where they rarely if ever saw their putative father. This was not a new situation.

In 1938 the British Government set up a Royal Commission to advise on how to deal with the apparent spread of 'promiscuity', which resulted in what was described as 'an organised campaign against the social, moral and economic evils of promiscuity'.[7] This included putting strong pressure upon couples living in faithful concubinage to marry. But the 'Mass Marriage Movement' launched in 1945 lasted only ten years. Initially the marriage rate rose but by 1951 it had dropped and the illegitimacy rate reverted to the earlier level. The attempt to impose Western nuclear family patterns upon West Indian working class and peasant society was doomed to failure as it was never based upon an understanding and appreciation of conjugal and mating practices that had developed over the centuries since Africans were forcibly introduced to the Caribbean islands.

9.4 Concubine Relationships

The impermanence of concubine relationships left an indelible effect upon the children. In the crowded confines of a small home they often witnessed the rows of their parents, and if the mother was abused, or if the man eventually left her, they would invariably take the side of the mother. She, and her mother, the children's grandmother, were seen as the stable units in family life. This created a predominantly matriarchal society.

The general concept in Jamaican society which has survived is that children are a 'woman's business' and when relationships break up the man usually feels under no obligation to contribute to the maintenance of the children he caused to be brought into the world. If the mother of his child pursues him he will feel aggrieved, and if she goes to court and obtains a maintenance order it would rarely be enforced as the sympathies of the legal authorities were with the man. It has become an institutionalised part of the culture that the man is free to have sexual relations wherever he can get them, but any children resulting from his actions are not his responsibility.

9.5 Fatherhood

R T Smith, in his analysis of family types among lower class West Indian families, went so far as to say that men were irrelevant in family life. He said:

Children derive nothing of any importance from their fathers, who are marginal and ineffective members of their families of procreation, even when resident. It is indeed indifferent whether these husband-fathers live with their families or not, or even whether their children know them personally.[8]

Smith believed that this male marginality in familial contexts derived from the low rates of social mobility, restricted public roles for adult men, and an absence of managerial functions, political responsibilities and status differentiation among the lower classes. He believed that the rigid colour code that kept black men in the lowest social class institutionalised their marginality, and this was all controlled by economic factors. His analysis centred upon the household as the natural unit of family organisation, from which he then asserted that common law unions and legal marriage are sociologically identical in lower class West Indian society.

Both Smith and Clarke based their analysis upon current economic and social conditions with no reference to the past. Henriques, by contrast, constantly referred to the period of colonial slavery and to characteristics that have their roots in West African society. He noted that a number of Africans on the plantations in Jamaica had come from the Ibo tribe and records stated that they were of a 'more gentle' disposition and were therefore often used in a household capacity in the great houses of the planters. African tribal society was essentially patriarchal and it was the social structure of slavery that changed this. Henriques notes that after the abolition of the slave trade in 1807 the planters encouraged promiscuity in the slave dormitories in order to produce as many children as possible as Africans could no longer be imported. The older women who were unable to do heavy work in the field gangs cared for the children and this established the matriarchal family unit in which grandmothers played a significant role in 1960s Jamaica.

The strongest recollection of their father that many boys carried over into adult life was that of indifference or neglect. If the woman was left destitute, her children would either be cared for by her mother, the children's grandmother, or, if that were not possible, they would be taken in by some other relative. Family and kinship ties have traditionally been strong in West Indian society and children are greatly valued. They are never subjected to discrimination due to their birth outside a stable family unit. Siblings may be split up and cared for by different relatives but if, at a later date, the mother's circumstances change, she may take them back into her new home, although if she is in a new relationship from which there are children she will rarely bring the children of her previous relationships into her new home.

The majority of emigrants to Britain in the 1950s and 1960s came from the working classes and rural peasant communities of Jamaica. The position of men in the social structure of these working class black communities was always unstable. Young men in family life would come and go, entering into more than one domestic arrangement, although they would usually eventually settle with one woman to give them comfort in their old age. These were the social customs and culture that were brought to Britain in the 1950s and 1960s. They were formative in the early days of the Black British African-Caribbean community and they are relevant for this present study.

9.6 Family Life among West Indian Immigrants in the UK in the 1950s and 1960s – Social Background

The emigration to Britain of West Indians, beginning in 1948, from the three main islands, Jamaica, Trinidad and Barbados, as well as from the smaller islands such as Montserrat, was largely an outcome of poverty in the colonial territories and the demand for labour in the booming economy of post–World War II Britain, as the nation sought to recover from wartime destruction and austerity. We have already noted the shock experienced by the migrants who came to Britain with unrealistic expectations of a warm welcome from the 'mother of the Commonwealth'. Just ten years after the *Empire Windrush* sailed up the Thames with the first handful of immigrants, the nation was shocked by the ferocity of race riots in Notting Hill and Nottingham — normally peaceful areas of London and the East Midlands.

Those who were not familiar with these areas were taken by surprise, but it was no surprise to the residents. There had been lots of press reports of the problems of overcrowding and culture clashes, but these were largely in local newspapers and they rarely hit the nationals. I had been living in west London not far from Notting Hill for a number of years prior to the riots, and I was well aware of the social tensions in the area. I had actually foretold the possibility of social disturbances in a book published in 1958.[9]

The general view among politicians and social commentators in the 1950s was that the immigration would not last long; it was a temporary social phenomenon of workers seeking employment to enable them to send money home to support their families and then to return home themselves. The early immigration was almost entirely of men seeking work, but by the end of the 1950s these early migrants had begun sending for their wives and sweethearts and it became increasingly clear that it was their intention to remain in Britain for a longer period and that what we were witnessing was the establishment of a permanent black minority in many of our major cities.

9.7 Immigration: a Political Issue

Politicians were jolted by the riots. They suddenly awoke to this new social phenomenon and realised that there were potentially hundreds of millions of British passport holders in the colonies who had a right to settle in Britain. Panic invaded Westminster and Whitehall. The aftermath of the Empire that had made Britain the foremost trading nation in the world was now perceived to be likely to destroy her. De-colonisation had created the Commonwealth which, alas, was founded upon imperialist and paternalist notions. Elspeth Huxley dryly commented that the Commonwealth was:

> ... an idea in minds that, like all human minds, recoils from uncongenial reality, such as the loss of power and glory, and wants to go on believing that as things were, so they remain. A sort of mummy case in which we have embalmed an Empire that's dead but that we can't

bring ourselves finally to bury, because we want to go on feeling that something is still there.[10]

It was not only in Parliament that arguments raged on what should be done to save Britain disappearing under the weight of millions of unwanted immigrants who would take our jobs, our girls and our homes, destroying the character of the nation. From the riots of 1958 the debates raged for ten years, climaxing in Enoch Powell's 'rivers of blood' speech in May 1968. This very public debate confirmed in the public's mind that black immigrants from the tropical Commonwealth were a 'problem' that had to be stopped, but nobody knew how to do it without destroying the Commonwealth and everything for which it stood.

The answer devised by the politicians was in the Commonwealth Immigrants Acts of 1962 and 1968 which effectively closed the door to the unrestricted entry of non-white people from the tropical 'new' Commonwealth while leaving the door open for white citizens of the 'old' Commonwealth — the Dominions such as Canada, Australia and New Zealand. The effect of this was to reinforce the old prejudices and attitudes of white superiority. Sheila Paterson said that mild xenophobia is a cultural norm among the British.

The attitude is one of avoidance rather than aggression and it applies not only to outsiders but to out-groups within the society, between North and South, between one village and another, even between neighbouring streets. It goes back over many centuries of village life, historical and cultural continuity and insular isolation.... The Englishman prefers the country to the town and home to foreign parts. He is rather glad and relieved if only natives will remain natives and strangers, and at a comfortable distance from himself.[11]

9.8 Immigration: a Social Issue

It would be untrue to give the impression that the difficulties of acceptance encountered by the West Indian immigrants were all due to racial prejudice among the British. We have already referred to their own unrealistic expectations of 'coming home', but by far the most significant factor was the physical environment of inner-city areas where they settled in large numbers. These areas already had a range of social problems which the presence of the immigrants exacerbated but did not create: housing shortage, substandard, ageing, decrepit properties, lack of amenities, and poverty.

This was not just a matter of concern for London. Birmingham City Corporation, in 1963, ran a campaign against 'Rachmanism' — the practice of letting substandard accommodation to tenants and grossly profiteering. In one case the City Corporation applied to compulsorily purchase fourteen terraced houses in Sparkbrook, housing 301 people (Indians, Pakistanis, English, Irish and West Indians) although the properties had been declared unfit for human habitation by the City's Medical Officer of Health.[12] In North Kensington and Paddington 'Rachmanism' was said to be flourishing in a newspaper report which gave a number of detailed case histories.[13] This report was just one of hundreds that appeared around this time confirming the dire state of many inner-city properties and their gross overcrowding. Although this was five years after the Notting Hill riots, these conditions still existed and demonstrated the difficulties that faced the first generation of immigrants.[14]

9.9 Family Life

The passing of the Commonwealth Immigrants Act 1962 had a profound effect, not only upon those in the West Indies who wanted to come to Britain, but upon those who were already here. It impacted attitudes, encouraging them to stay in Britain as they might not get back in if they did not settle back home. Until this time it was the intention of the vast majority of the immigrants in Britain to return home after a few years of work in Britain, but the public discussion of the impending restrictions upon immigration that began in the late1950s changed their perspective and caused them to bring their women to this country and to form family units. Net immigration from the West Indies was only 15,000 in 1958 and 16,400 in 1959, with almost as many returning to the Caribbean as emigrated to Britain. The following year there were large numbers of women and children among the almost 50,000 immigrants.

This does not mean that all dependants were brought to Britain by the early immigrants: quite the reverse, large numbers of dependants were left behind in the West Indies, particularly the children of common law unions. In the twenty year period from 1948 to 1968 some 300,000 migrants from the West Indies came to the UK. The effect upon family life, both in the West Indies and in Britain, was chaotic. I saw for myself some of the effects of the migration in Jamaica in 1962. The following year I described what I had seen:

A very large number of children have been left behind in the West Indies. This is, in fact, one of the saddest features of the migration. The breakup of family life is causing grave social problems for those responsible for community and moral welfare in the Caribbean. Children who have been left in the care of ageing grandmothers are often sorely neglected, as are others who have been left with aunts or cousins or even friends.[15]

9.10 Effects in the Caribbean

Before continuing to trace the development of family life in the West Indian migrant communities in Britain, it is

171

relevant to record what I wrote in 1963 about the effects of the migration upon family life in Jamaica:

> I have discussed the problems of the 'backwash' of the migration with many social workers in Jamaica as well as having seen for myself the sad and often deplorable state of these children who have been deprived of the love and security as well as the care and attention of their parents. A senior Jamaican welfare worker spoke of the migration to Britain as 'the greatest tragedy Jamaica has ever suffered'. He went on to say that he felt that migration was responsible for the 'final breakup of Jamaican family life'.[16]

I believe he was taking a very pessimistic view under the stress of the many problems facing workers in his department. Nevertheless the fact remained that a very large number of children and young people were growing up in the West Indies who had forgotten what their parents even looked like and who were running wild for the lack of parental control. I further wrote:

> Many migrants indeed are in no position to send for their children. Often, as soon as the wife arrives in this country she begins to rear another family here. Owing to the overcrowded housing conditions which all the immigrants have to face they cannot possibly undertake the additional burden of bringing over their older children.[17]

The wide range of social problems created in Jamaica by the twenty year period of emigration are still to be seen today in the poverty, the shambolic family life, the social and political tensions and the severe economic depression of twenty-first century Jamaica. The 'beautiful land of wood and water' is still suffering from three hundred years of colonial exploitation, the aftermath of slavery, and under-investment.

9.11 Struggle for Survival

The West Indian immigrants struggling for survival in the depressed inner-city areas of Britain in the 1950s and 1960s were hugely brave in contending with the difficulties they faced. It was an unequal battle with all too little help from the authorities, ignorance and prejudice in the general public, and terrible living conditions. **"Sorry: No Coloured"** was the banner that greeted them in the adverts for rooms or flats to let, on every street corner shop and in the local papers. They had only their own determination, and tiny collective resources through sharing and helping one another in desperate times, to carry them through. Throughout the period of settlement of the first generation of migrants I visited hundreds of homes where I saw the poverty and hardship being endured, like the single mother who had been deserted by her partner and was struggling to feed her child and herself. Under current rates of National Assistance in 1963, an unmarried mother with one child and no employment or other means of support, received fifty-seven shillings and sixpence a week (£2.87) for the mother and 18 shillings (£0.90) for the child. The Board would pay the whole of what they considered to be a 'reasonable' rent. But they insisted upon the accommodation being furnished, with proof that the rent was being paid. Under the 1957 Rent Act it was incumbent upon the landlord to provide the tenant with a rent book. Many landlords, however, refused to do this as it would reveal their income to the Inland Revenue (HMRC) and they would have to pay tax on their rents.

Jamaican immigrants had never paid tax before coming to Britain and they resented the Government taking what they believed was rightly theirs. If the tenant reported them they would simply terminate the tenancy and evict the luckless tenant onto the street, there being no legal protection for tenants of furnished rooms at that time. West Indian single mothers knew that they would not find another room. They were too proud to beg, so they went without food themselves to feed the child. There was no other help in those days for the real poverty and hunger endured by many of the first generation immigrants. Any help came from voluntary groups who slowly became aware of the problems being experienced by the newcomers. My own church was a leader in this field. At first we did not realise that we were doing anything unique — we were simply responding to the local situation and people in need. Then the media discovered us. But the publicity we were given helped to encourage others to look at the situation in their own locality.

9.12 Marriage and Common Law Unions

Family life in the first generation was a mixture. I wrote about this in 1958, describing the plight of the young woman in a concubine relationship in Jamaica who scraped together the boat fare with borrowed money to come to England.

> She sets out on her new life, full of good intentions and perhaps gets a job in a biscuit factory and shares a room with another coloured girl and is thus able to send home £2.00 or £3.00 a week to support her family.[18]

She then formed a relationship with a man in Britain and they lived together. There was no question of them practising birth control as this was before the days of the contraceptive pill becoming popular in Britain. Moreover, Jamaicans had never been used to practising any kind of birth control in the Caribbean, which they considered contrary to nature and to the will of God. When she became pregnant and had to cease work, she could no longer afford to send money home to support her children or her aged mother, so her new situation was a tragedy for them as well as increasing hardship for herself.

One of two things would then happen. First: if the couple

were following the tradition they had learned back home they would simply continue to live together in a common law union. This left the young mother in a vulnerable situation because such unions had no recognition in British law.[19] It was highly likely that the man would live with her for a time and then his fancies would turn elsewhere, particularly in the last weeks of her pregnancy and the time of adjusting to a new baby in the house. If he was not getting the sexual satisfaction that he wished, he would find it elsewhere as was the custom in the Caribbean. He would set up another household and it was highly likely that he would make no contribution to his former partner and their child, or, if he paid her an allowance for a short time, there was no long-term commitment to such support.

Secondly: if the couple had a sufficiently strong personal relationship and commitment to each other, they would decide that the time had come to acknowledge this by marriage. They would then seek a church where they would book a wedding, either before or after the woman had given birth, and they would send invitations to their friends and acquaintances. Their guests would all come, not only from the local migrant community, but they would include kin from far and wide who came to join in the festivities. There would certainly be no approbation if the bride was obviously pregnant.

There would be no honeymoon but a lot would be spent on the provision of food in the house, and music and dancing would go on throughout the evening and late into the night, sometimes much to the annoyance of local white English residents. This was all part of the community tensions in the early days of the settlement of migrants in inner-city areas. But gradually the different communities adjusted to each other and accommodated cultural differences. It seemed to me that most of the West Indian couples in London were getting married, because I was regularly marrying five or six couples on a Saturday. I knew that Register Office weddings were not popular with the migrants. If they were going to get married they would do it 'properly' and have a full church service which would mark their rise in social status in the same way as marriage did in the West Indies. Photographs of the wedding were greatly prized. These were sent back to their families at home as proofs of their rise in social status. But some research I did for the Institute of Race Relations in 1963 revealed that in churches of all denominations across the area covered by the old London County Council there were only 1,564 church weddings during the twelve months ending 31 March 1963. This was at a time when the 1961 census had revealed that there were 70,488 West Indian immigrants residing in the same area.

Of course, an unknown number of them were already married, but this was a time when the migrant community was settling into family units, and after July 1962 those who wished to bring girlfriends or common law wives to the UK had to classify them as 'fiancées'. They then had three months in which to marry or the woman would be classified as an 'illegal immigrant' and face deportation. This often put an unrealistic pressure upon the couple as they both needed to work in order to save sufficient money to pay for the wedding and the feast for their friends and kin.

The practice of marrying 'whiter' continued in Britain as a social aspiration, but as late as 1973 a research report in the Journal of the Community Relations Commission said, 'Racially mixed marriages in Britain appear to be quite rare.'[20] In 1964 I had been the adviser for an Independent Television programme on mixed marriages and I had scoured London for racially mixed couples. Their stories of the prejudice and hardship they encountered, prior to the first Race Relations Act 1965, were not only revealing for those who dared to break the great 'mixed-sex' taboo, but also for showing how little integration had taken place between the first generation of migrants and the white host society. This underlines the veracity of the Third Generation Theory which states that the first-generation migrants rarely mix with members of the host society.[21]

9.13 Fatherhood

We have already noted that West Indian marriage customs largely derived from the time of colonial slavery where paternal responsibilities were virtually non-existent. This carried over into continuing male inability to provide sufficient support, which produced complex patterns of serial monogamy amongst women, and matrifocal family structures in which the children quite commonly had different fathers. This culture of family life carried over into the migrant communities in Britain in the 1960s. Up until 1955 the majority of those coming to Britain were single males. Thereafter, in some years, women outnumbered men, most of them being single or common law wives coming to join their partner.

In Jamaica a concubine household was matriarchal. Children were the woman's business and she not only dealt with their physical needs but she was also responsible for discipline. The man rarely had much to do with the children, but, if the couple married, the man expected to take his place as head of the family and to take responsibility for disciplining the children, especially in serious matters. His methods of physical punishment would often be quite severe, taking his belt off to both boys and girls. In the migrant communities in Britain the same culture prevailed in family life in the 1950s and 1960s with the first generation of settlers. Relationships between children and their fathers were often either distant or strained.

The first generation of children born in this country suffered grave disadvantage. They not only lived in a two world dichotomy, having to cope with two conflicting worldviews — that of their peer group in school, and that of their parents' in the home — but they also felt unsupported, not understood and insecure. Discipline in the home, as we have observed, was often very strict, being of the standard experienced by their parents in the West Indies, which increased their sense of alienation from their parents and the cultural milieu that they represented. They felt even more devastated and alone in a strange world of conflicting cultures when their father left home. In those days family breakdown in the UK was quite rare, so when the West Indian child was left alone with his mother this increased his social distance from his peer group at school and in the neighbourhood.

David Lammy MP movingly describes his own experience of life in Tottenham when his father left home and he was aged twelve. He never saw him again. He writes:

> In Peterborough, where I had won a choral scholarship, things were different. There I was far more self-conscious about the stigma surrounding our family. Why did I have one parent, not two, sitting next to me at parents' evenings? Why was only my mum watching me in the school play? Why was it that everybody else had a father shouting their name on sports day? ... There were many moments when I struggled to cope with what I felt like betrayal by my father.... Without her husband, my mother fought desperately hard to hold her family together, reaching deep into a formative black cultural experience that relied heavily on faith and self-help. My siblings and I would be at church on a Sunday, perfectly turned out, whether we liked it or not.[22]

David Lammy is certainly right in speaking of the fortitude of his mother and her self-sacrificial commitment to her family. He says that his mother worked non-stop, doing two and sometimes three jobs in order to pay the mortgage, the insurance, and provide for her children. In this she was not unique. My own personal experience of thousands of the immigrants confirms this. Indeed, his mother's indomitable spirit was typical of the first generation of immigrants from the West Indies. They came with a very strong work ethic, determined to find employment, to send money back home to support those who had sacrificially helped them to emigrate and to raise their own standard of living.

The first generation, both men and women, had strong commitments to fulfilling family responsibilities. The bitter experience of life in Britain, and the devastating disappointment, crushing their hopes and dreams, had a greater effect upon the men. The women were more resilient, no doubt due to their socialisation in the West Indies and their total commitment to their children. The fact that in some households the strong work ethic of the first generation was not passed on to the second and third generations has to be seen in the context of the hostile social environment which greeted them, and their struggles for survival which many found unbearable in much the same way as MP David Lammy's father, who resorted to drink after his business collapsed.

9.14 Youth
David Lammy's personal experience was replicated in the lives of thousands of young people in the West Indian communities growing up in the inner-city areas up and down the country. Studies showed that the West Indian child suffered more than Indian and Pakistani children in the Hindu and Muslim communities in the UK. West Indian migrants brought with them a culture dominated for the past three hundred years by British customs and traditions of language,

179

education, law and religion. Everything British was revered. The Asian child also lived in a two world dichotomy, but when he or she encountered rejection in relationships with white children they were able to retreat into the security of the distinctive traditional culture of their parents. The West Indian child had no such consolation where he could find a sense of belonging and security so essential to personal stability.

My own research in London confirmed this. In 1969 I wrote:

> The West Indian child born in Britain is socialised in the 'pop culture'. He has the local accent, he shares the same taste in music and dress; he has the same social and economic aspirations as local white children, he has played with them since he was five and they started together in the same primary school. He has visited their homes, been to their parties, eaten with them, played with them, romped in the park, fought in the playground, competed on the sports field with them, and then suddenly, when they reach their teens, a change in their relationship takes place. When his friends begin courting they do not want to know him. They no longer invite him into their homes where he might meet their sisters. When they meet him in the street they avoid him. He is no longer one of them. He is baffled, hurt and unhappy. It is a short step from this to being angry, to hating white society and all that it stands for, to hating the world and everything and everyone in it.[23]

A report from Birmingham in 1963 similarly showed that there was no lasting integration:

> A West Indian boy said, 'as soon as you leave school you go one way and the white boys go another.' Teachers commented that prejudice grew as school leaving age approached: 'there appears to be very little integration. Toleration, acceptance, some respect for each other's abilities and personal qualities, amicable relationships, team

partnership and an occasional friendship — but little more.' With rare exceptions, integration had failed in the youth clubs, despite strenuous efforts. West Indians felt unwelcome in white clubs and dance halls.... The young second-generation West Indians seem the most likely candidates for the role of tomorrow's depressed citizens, with their colour consciousness, their shifting family life and their voluntary or involuntary segregation in potential Harlems.[24]

The Times commented upon this report:

Will the West Indian community take a good hard look at the way it is bringing up its children? One thing is certain. Almost nobody believes that the thousands of coloured Britons in Birmingham schools have an equal chance in the life ahead of them.[25]

This was a perceptive comment, acknowledging the difficulty that any child in those communities would have in breaking free from its consequences. But it was a purely negative comment, offering no solution — not calling for action to change the hostile social environment. It appeared to put all the blame upon West Indian parents and accepted no responsibility on the part of the host society. This was in some way analogous to other cases of the victim being blamed for creating the circumstances that contributed to his own suffering. The most depressing feature of *The Times* report back in 1963 was that there appeared to be an almost universally accepted inevitability that things were bad and could only get worse for West Indian inner-city communities. No-one in either local or national government appeared to be paying attention to the warning signs. The seeds were sown right there which would result in the riots of August 2011.

FREE AT LAST?

Notes

[1] T S Simey, *Welfare and Planning in the West Indies*, Oxford University Press, London, 1946, pp. 82–83.

[2] F Henriques, *Family and Colour in Jamaica*, MacGibbon and Kee, London 1953, p. 109.

[3] R T Smith, *The Negro Family in British Guiana*, Routledge, Keegan Paul, London, 1956.

[4] Edith Clarke, *My Mother Who Fathered Me*, University of the West Indies Press, Kingston, Jamaica, 1957.

[5] Edith Clarke, *op. cit.*, pp. 65–66.

[6] *Ibid.*, p. 2.

[7] West India Royal Commission Report, London, HMSO, 1945, Command 6607, pp. 220–222.

[8] R T Smith, T*he Negro Family in British Guiana*, p. 147: quoted by M.G. Smith in the Introduction to *'My Mother Who Fathered Me'* p. xxviii.

[9] *Black and White in Harmony, op. cit.*

[10] Elspeth Huxley, *Backstreet New Worlds – a Look at Immigrants in Britain*, Chatto and Windus, London, 1964, pp. 152–3.

[11] Sheila Paterson, *Racial Images and Attitudes in Britain – The Background* – in *Race a Christian Symposium*, Eds. Clifford Hill and David Matthews, Gollancz, London, 1968, p. 67.

[12] Reported in *The Times,* 5 September 1963.

[13] *The Guardian,* 27 September 1963.

[14] 49,650 immigrants from the West Indies arrived in Britain during 1960. The following year 66,300 came in, and a further 31,800 arrived in the first six months of 1962 before the Commonwealth Immigrants Act came into force on 1 July. Thus 147,750 arrived in 2 ½ years. But this was not the driving force behind the legislation because the total population of Jamaica was less than two million. It was fear of vast numbers from India and Pakistan. Immigration from Pakistan had leapt from 850 in 1959 to 25,100 in 1961; and from India there were 2,950 in 1959 increasing to 23,750 in 1961.

[15] Clifford Hill, *West Indian Migrants and the London Churches*, Oxford University Press, London, 1963, p. 40.

[16] *Ibid.*, p. 40.

[17] *Ibid.*, p. 41.

[18] Clifford Hill, *Black and White in Harmony*, Hodder, London, 1958, p. 56.

[19] National Assistance Board did not recognise the validity of dependant responsibilities in the Caribbean so they would not pay for any money to be sent back home.

[20] *New Community: Journal of the Community Relations Commission*, Autumn 1973, p. 337.

[21] See section 9.13.

[22] David Lammy, *Out of the Ashes – Britain After the Riots*, Guardian Books, 2011, London, pp. 98–100.

[23] Clifford Hill, *Immigration and Integration, A Study of the Settlement of Coloured Minorities in Britain*, Pergamon Press, Oxford, 1970, pp. 138–9.

[24] Institute of Race Relations, Newsletter, December 1963, pp. 6–7.

[25] *The Times*, 7 November 1963.

Chapter Ten

FAMILY AND CULTURE (PART 2)

10.1 The Family in Britain from the 1950s

If we are to reach a fully rounded understanding of the range of social influences bearing upon the first and second generations of Caribbeans in Britain, we have to take account of the forces of social change driving what, in the 1950s and 1960s, was euphemistically called 'the host society'.

10.2 The Social Environment

Since the days of the Industrial Revolution, family life in working class urban communities in Britain remained largely socially static until after the Second World War, with very little opportunity for advanced education and social mobility. The Education Act of 1944 was a milestone in creating opportunities for many of the brighter children of working class origins. It institutionalised the 11–plus examination, whereby some children were selected for grammar schools and technical schools while the remainder went to secondary modern schools. It also raised the school leaving age from fourteen to fifteen, which came into force in 1947. The school leaving age was further raised to sixteen in 1972, where it remained until the Education and Skills Act 2008, which requires students to continue in education or training to the age of seventeen from 2013 and to eighteen from 2015.

Back in the 1940s there was only a limited number of grammar schools, with fewer in the north of England than the south and more boys' schools than girls', so places were restricted, but the 1944 Act recognised the need for increasing the educational opportunities for all children regardless of gender or social background. This provided the first step towards the social equality of women and laid the foundation for the sweeping social changes that would take place during the rest of the century. Further ground-breaking legislation also occurred in the 1940s. There were three major Acts establishing the Welfare State: the Family Allowance Act 1945, the National Insurance Act 1946, and the National Health Act 1948.

10.3 The Social Conservatism of the 1950s

The twentieth century was a highly formative period of social development in Britain but the post-World War II period was not only a time of creative social innovation, it was also marked by a strong social conservatism. There is no agreement among historians and sociologists as to the cause of this intensely conservative mood in the nation. Many historians simply note it as a time of reaction to the turmoil of the war years and a desire for the familiar patterns of family life when men were the breadwinners and women stayed at home to care for the children and to have a meal ready for their husbands.

Post-war reconstruction triggered a demand for labour and an economic boom which created higher wages than the working classes had ever enjoyed, while Retail Price Maintenance and rationing kept the cost of living stable. It also encouraged a higher birth rate, which tended to increase female domesticity and to decrease their participation in the labour market. Middle class women dutifully left behind their war work and resumed traditional domestic roles, while working class women learned to combine paid employment and home-based domestic work. For both social groups the production of labour saving devices designed to take the drudgery out of household chores became important.

The media in the late 1940s and throughout the 1950s reinforced the social ideal of marriage and the woman's place in the home. The huge progress towards gender equality in the war years, when women had to assume many of the jobs usually done by men, was put on hold. Women's magazines concentrated on motherhood, cookery and gardening, with romantic stories of women finding their soulmate, marrying, having a family and living happily ever after. It was an age of virtue and moral responsibility, when churchgoing reached its peak and church growth had never been so high since the 1870s.

It was as though, in reaction to the social chaos of two world wars and the deep economic recession of the 1930s, the nation wanted to return to the safety of social values that had undergirded what many saw as the golden age of Victorian prosperity. Throughout Britain more than half of the nation's children went to Sunday School in 1955, and each day schools began with an act of Christian worship, with the majority of children also being given at least a weekly period of 'Christian Education', which was mainly biblical with an emphasis upon standards of personal and social morality.

Traditional values of family, marriage, home and piety were central on the national agenda, from the end of the war to 1960. The visits of the American evangelist Billy Graham drew vast crowds in football stadia and other mass venues, with almost two million people attending the 1954 London meetings, and 1.2 million the 1955 Scottish meetings. Children's uniformed organisations thrived, with Brownies and Guides, Cubs and Scouts, being taught conservative social values of politeness, honesty and service, doing 'Bob-a-Job weeks' and holding 'Purpose Days'.

10.4 The Shock of the 1960s

All this cosy social conservatism came to a sudden and violent end in the 1960s. It took many people by surprise, although there had been portents as early as 1955 with the advent of Bill Haley's *Rock around the Clock*, which introduced a style of music new to many young people, resulting in a new phenomenon of youth mob violence when teenage cinema-goers danced in the aisles and ripped up the seats in the Empire Theatre, Elephant and Castle, in south-east London. The youth music part of Western society's 'Cultural Revolution' was on!

Callum Brown summarised this period of rapid social change:

> In the 1960s, the institutional structures of cultural traditionalism started to crumble in Britain: the ending of the worst excesses of moral censorship (notably after the 1960 trial of *Lady Chatterley's Lover* and the ending in 1968 of the Lord Chamberlain's control over British theatre); the legalisation of abortion (1967) and homosexuality (1967), and the granting of easier divorce (1969); the emergence of the women's liberation movement, especially from 1968; the flourishing of youth culture centred on popular music (especially after the emergence of the Beatles in late 1962) and incorporating a range of cultural pursuits and identities (ranging from the widespread use of drugs to the fashion revolution); and the appearance of student rebellion (notably between 1968 and the early 1970s).[1]

It was a breathtaking period of social change, with an immediate effect upon social values: institutional change would soon follow. Sociologists in this period recognised five major social institutions in advanced urban industrial societies. They were: **the family, the economy, education, the law and religion**. It was recognised that when changes took place in any one of these institutions all the others were affected. The 1960s witnessed a unique sociological phenomenon in which each of its major social institutions was experiencing change *sui generis* and each was at the same time being affected by change in the other major social institutions. This created an extremely volatile situation of rapid social change. The first major social institution to experience radical change was the family, but changes within the family were soon institutionalised as they were reflected in legislation such as divorce reform. Changes in the family were closely followed by changes in education, the economy and the church. Thus by the end of the 1960s all five major social institutions were experiencing fundamental changes.

10.5 The Era of Change
Easier divorce triggered the crumbling of the traditional marriage-based family that had undergirded the stability of the nation for centuries. The relaxing of discipline within the home soon affected education, where changes were accelerated by a new breed of teachers trained in the post-war period with new methods of education moving away from learning by rote to encouraging students to discover for themselves, which required the relaxation of some classroom discipline, and also impacted general school discipline. The post-war economic boom was hugely influential in promoting the cultural change from age to youth. School leavers could move straight into well-paid employment, which created a new class of consumers with high earning power and low social responsibilities. The market quickly responded with the production of electronic devices and fashion goods, all aimed at young people.

Churchgoing began to fall in the 1960s with the end of petrol rationing and the increasing prosperity of the nation, which stimulated car ownership and weekend travel. The 1970s saw the collapse of afternoon Sunday Schools and the beginning of the decline in Christian education in day schools. At the same time the inflow of Asian immigrants with non-Christian religions brought multiculturalism into many schools, which affected the teaching of traditional Christian values.

What began in the 1960s as a few legal changes to enable the smooth functioning of society in a time of adjusting to the post-war world became a full-scale social revolution running through the 1970s as changes within each social institution affected each of the others. Once set in motion, the social revolution gathered momentum through to the end of the twentieth century and beyond. It shows no sign of ending in the second decade of the twenty-first century.

10.6 Results of the Social Revolution

Of all the social changes since the 1960s, the decline in family life has been the most influential. The annual number of first-time marriages in the early post-war period continued to rise until 1970 when it peaked at 340,000. By the end of the twentieth century they had dropped to less than half, at 170,000. The 2001 national census showed the total number of marriages (including remarriages) in England and Wales as 249,227. This was the lowest number of marriages recorded since 1897 despite a huge increase in population. At the same time the divorce rate rose steeply from 27,000 in 1961 to 260,000 in 2001, dropping to 119,000 in 2011, but this drop reflected the lower number of marriages.

The dramatic changes in family life in the second half of the twentieth century can best be illustrated by the percentage of babies born outside the marriage-based family, especially when this is viewed over an extended period of time. From parish records going back to the sixteenth century it can be seen that the number of children born out of marriage averaged around 4% of the total infant population. This was maintained for more than three centuries and throughout the first half of the twentieth century, with the exception of a blip during the Second World War when births outside marriage increased slightly to 6%. This returned to 4% by 1950. A slow rise began in 1960, continuing for the next twenty years and reaching 12% in 1980. From then until the present day the rise has been steep, year on year, taking it to almost 50% in 2012 (53% in Wales and in North East England).

Statistics from the 1960s through to the present day also show a steep rise in the number of one-parent families in the UK, most of whom are mothers caring for children in the absence of a father. While it needs to be stressed that many single mothers succeed, often self-sacrificially, in bringing up their children to responsible adulthood, others are not so fortunate. There is overwhelming statistical evidence to show that the majority of children involved in juvenile crime come from dysfunctional families. Of the 60,000 children who live in state care homes, 98% are admitted due to family breakdown.

Dysfunctional families are not necessarily those of single mothers —many are reconstituted families where children have to learn to live with their mother's new partner and other siblings, which often places enormous psychological strains upon sensitive children. Of the 100,000 children who run away from home every year in the UK, the majority come from this type of family, and it is in this type of family that many children are at risk of being physically and sexually abused.

Additionally, there is overwhelming evidence to show that children from broken families also suffer from poverty, ill-health, lower levels of educational attainment, substance and alcohol misuse, and early sexual activity including higher levels of sexually transmitted infections and teenage pregnancy. The evidence of the damage inflicted upon children by dysfunctional families is now incontrovertible and needs to be seen as a direct result of the social revolution that has taken place since the middle of the twentieth century.

There is an enormous cost to family breakdown. Its cost in terms of human suffering is incalculable, but in terms of the national economy it is estimated to cost the nation £40 billion a year through the support of single parent families, the health problems that are a direct result of the trauma of family breakdown, the provision of additional housing, the legal costs of separation and divorce, the additional cost of services provided by social services and welfare agencies, plus the knock-on effects in employment, child support and a multitude of other outcomes.

10.7 Social Drivers behind the Revolution

It is worth noting that the vast social changes that have taken place in Britain and other Western nations since the middle of the twentieth century have not simply been the outcome of the slow processes of social change that might be expected in any advanced society where knowledge is increasing and technological advances are continuing. The processes of social change have also been generated by those who have ideological agendas. As early as 1946, Dr Brock-Chisholm, who was the first Director of the World Health Organisation, said:

> The concept of right and wrong is a barrier to developing a civilised way of life. This concept of right and wrong should be eradicated. Children have to be freed from prejudices forced upon them by the religious authorities. Parents are dictators and the suppressors of the child's best nature.... Sex education should be introduced, eliminating 'the ways of the elders', by force if necessary.[2]

Secular humanists have been active in social engineering through all the mainline political parties since the 1960s and have had a strong influence upon the formation of Government social policy. Their influence has also been seen in fiscal legislation, where disincentives to marriage have accumulated. The legal and tax systems have operated as a disincentive to marriage.[3] Additionally, a small number of homosexuals of both genders have also been involved in promoting social change deliberately aimed at weakening traditional family life. In 1972 the London group of the Gay Liberation Front published a Manifesto in which they stated that: 'The family as the source of our oppression must be eliminated'. The Manifesto advocated a Communist style social structure in which the traditional nuclear family of a mother and father with their children would be replaced by people living in interchangeable relationships and children being cared for by groups rather than by their biological parents. Their attack upon the traditional family was further strengthened in 1979 with another Manifesto statement:

> The oppression of gay people starts in the most basic unit of society, the family, consisting of the man in charge, a slave as his wife, and their children on whom they force themselves as the ideal models. The very form of the family works against homosexuality.... We must aim at the abolition of the family.[4]

In addition to the ideological campaigners there have been some powerful commercial drivers behind the social revolution. It is not within the scope of this chapter to deal adequately with a vast array of commercial institutions, but in order to acknowledge the extent of their influence we note the following list: the illegal drugs and substance pushers, the music industry, the drinks trade, the pornography vendors, the computer games industry, the video/DVD/film moguls, the sex 'education' promoters, the IT and mobile phones industry and the wide ranging fashion industry. All of these have been drivers with massive commercial interests in exploiting children and vulnerable young people and have been influential innovators and beneficiaries in the social revolution.

10.8 The Arts and the Media

The arts and the media, which are major social institutions, have both played a significant part in influencing public opinion through popularising the 'permissive society' where violence and adultery are commonplace in television soaps and other programmes watched by millions. Teenage magazines have remorselessly presented sexual relationships without responsibility or commitment, and pornography has flooded the internet, even reaching into the lives of quite young children who have access through their computers, mobile phones and other IT devices.

From about 2010 the practice of 'sexting' among teenagers rapidly gained acceptance as young people took pictures on their mobile phones of themselves naked and used the social media to transmit these images to their friends. They are, of course, accessible to children of any age. Once these images are in circulation there is no control on where they can appear across the world wide web. Apart from their potential to corrupt a whole generation of young people, these images can be used for bullying and blackmail. Those who expose themselves in this way may bitterly regret it in later years when they find the images are still available.

Many observers of the twenty-first century social scene believe that the most powerful influence upon the lives of young people comes from the music they listen to and the computer games they play. The rap songs, often with messages of rebellion against the values of wider society, and some even with incitement to rape and other forms of violent abuse including advocating suicide, are listened to by millions of young people. Through social networks they come together at predetermined venues where alcohol and drugs are available.

Findings from an NHS survey in England in 2009 found that a quarter of a million children had taken drugs during the previous month, and around 450,000 had taken drugs during the previous year. Surveys also indicate that there is a strong link between sexual behaviour and the use of drugs and alcohol leading to the vast increase in sexually transmitted infections in the past decade. According to the NHS, the incidence of STIs among teenagers has reached 'epidemic proportions'.

10.9 Fragmentation of Family Life

The outcome of the multi-directional attack upon marriage and traditional family life has been disastrous for the national economy, for law and order, for the health of the nation and for the stability of its social structure. Dennis Wrigley, the leader of the Maranatha Community, summarised the consequences of the social revolution at a conference in the House of Commons in October 2006:

"It is beyond dispute that moral values are learnt primarily within the family. When parental influence is undermined and the educational system is used as a means of social engineering, the influence of the family unit is seriously eroded. The increasing rejection of private and public morality has led to a dangerous situation in which children do not see issues in terms of right and wrong, but rather in terms of preference. Reference to absolute truth is rejected. Those with strong convictions are automatically labelled as intolerant. Agnosticism is always seen as superior to belief. Many of those concerned with movements for social change rooted in secular humanism have been staunch in their rejection of marriage and often family and do not believe that children should have the advantage of learning from the experience of previous generations, notably through their family." [5]

The overwhelming evidence from numerous studies shows that the single most influential factor in the present situation among young people is the fragmentation of family life. Nearly a quarter of the nation's children live with only one parent.[6] Almost half of all children born today will experience the breakdown of their parents' relationship.[7] 200,000 children had one parent in prison at some point in 2009.[8] A report from the Centre for Social Justice stated:

> The majority of young offenders come from broken homes, nearly two-thirds have drug and alcohol addiction problems, more than three in four have no educational qualifications and many young prisoners have mental health problems rooted in drug abuse. Broken families are often the places where the seeds are sown for future criminal activity.[9]

10.10 Background to the Riots

In view of the overwhelming evidence from a multitude of social surveys, it is hardly surprising that young people took advantage of the protest of Mark Duggan's family. They were ignored by senior police officers when they went to make a polite inquiry concerning the circumstances surrounding reports that he had been shot by police officers. Subsequent events show that the police were not only taken by surprise, they were totally unprepared for what happened. This was a situation where the community police should have been aware of the tensions in the community. In my own experience, outbreaks of community violence are never totally spontaneous. They are the outcome of a build-up of tension over a period of many months or years. Usually the signs of that build-up can be seen by community workers who are familiar with the area. It is difficult to know why they were not known to the police, and measures taken to reduce the tension.

But the underlying causes of the riots go back a lot

farther than the few months prior to the summer of 2011. Throughout the earlier chapters of this book we have been tracing the roots of social alienation among both Caribbean and white British young people. Indeed the roots of family breakdown were there in the migrant communities before the social revolution began in British cities. The roots lay in the working class communities back in the West Indian islands, with their strong matriarchal traditions which left men free to have multiple relationships. The first wave of migrants coming to Britain in the late 1940s and throughout the 1950s were keen to be accepted among their white workmates. Most of them adopted the local culture and married their girlfriends and common law spouses soon after their arrival in Britain. In the early 1960s this was actually encouraged by immigration law which readily granted entry to fiancées but required them to marry within three months of their arrival.

Certainly there were plenty of stresses and strains within the family life of first-generation migrants who faced severe hardships especially in terms of housing and employment. By the middle of the 1960s family breakdown in the Caribbean communities was not uncommon. By this time, however, there were other social pressures. The British social revolution had begun. The new affluence among white people in working class communities rapidly changed social values and triggered high rates of consumer consumption, with parents who had grown up with wartime austerity determined to give their children all the things that they had never had. Traditional discipline within the home collapsed in many families as parents reacted against the harsh discipline they had suffered from their parents, which resulted in increased levels of behavioural problems among young people.

The outcomes of the social revolution that we have been tracing in this chapter had their effect upon the migrant communities. This was the social environment into which the first generation of migrants from the West Indies settled. The social revolution undoubtedly had its effect which combined with relationship stress in Caribbean households and led to an increasing rate of marriage breakdown, although many in this first generation held on to the social and personal values which they had brought with them. This was particularly so for those who had a strong Christian faith, even for those who were unable to find fellowship in local churches. Their faith survived the impact of migration. But it was the second generation who were hugely affected by the social revolution in Britain. In accordance with Third Generation Theory outlined in Chapter 5 they would be expected to conform to the host society social values. The influence of their peer group with whom they were educated in school and among whom they lived in the neighbourhood was paramount over the values of their parents in their homes.

In many inner-city urban neighbourhoods there was a shared sense of relative deprivation among both black and white young people who through advertising and the media were constantly made aware of the affluence of young people in other areas and of their own relative poverty. The sense of injustice generated by their circumstances and their lack of opportunity to achieve, due to poor educational attainment and low social ranking, resulted in antisocial attitudes and dissipated any effort to succeed.

It was this shared sense of relative deprivation bringing black and white young people together, which was a powerful force behind the inner-city riots which began in Tottenham on 6 August 2011. It is contended in this book that the roots of this relative deprivation can be traced back to the experience of 'colonial slavery' in the black community and industrial 'white slavery' in the white community. These are powerful social drivers which have never been adequately recognised or steps taken to eradicate them. On the contrary, both forms of slavery were expunged from educational curricula in Britain for two hundred years and hidden from public view as though they did not happen. Until they are faced, and steps taken towards reconciliation, they will continue as a running sore in British society that will break open from time to time.

If these steps are not taken we will undoubtedly see riots in British cities once again at some time in the future. It is inevitable unless there is a radical change in the social dynamics of power in our inner-city communities. The sombre truth is that Government policy since the beginning of the economic crisis in 2008 has been fixated upon the economy: bringing in foreign investment; measures to stimulate home ownership to get the housing market moving; stimulating small business growth by encouraging bank loans; and many other economic initiatives. But social change is not high on the political agenda. Until attention is given to the plight of the powerless in inner-city ghettos of deprivation, the day of reckoning will surely come.

Notes

[1] Callum G. Brown, *The Death of Christian Britain, Understanding Secularisation 1800–2000*, Routledge, London, p. 176.

[2] Psychiatry of Enduring Peace and Social Progress, *Psychiatry*, Vol. 9, 1946.

[3] Some small tax advantage for married couples was announced by the Government in September 2013.

[4] Gay Liberation Front Manifesto, 1979. Quoted in the *Big Question: What on earth are we doing to our Children?* The Maranatha Community, December 2012.

[5] Dennis Wrigley, *Marriage and Family in the United Kingdom – An Overview*, The Maranatha Community, Flixton, Manchester, October 2006.

[6] Office of National Statistics, 2012.

[7] Centre for Social Justice, May 2012.

[8] Ministry of Justice, 2012.

[9] Centre for Social Justice, 2007.

Chapter Eleven

SOCIAL INEQUALITY

In this chapter we must now bring together, summarise and apply some of our earlier observations.

11.1 TUC Conference

The riots which swept through English cities in August 2011 revealed 'deep fractures' in British society and underlined the 'folly of Coalition policy', so claimed the leader of the Trades Union Congress (TUC), Brendan Barber, when he addressed their three-day annual conference in September 2011. He said:

> "What happened in August actually revealed deep fractures within our society – a society that ranks among the most unequal anywhere in the developed world, where a super-rich elite have been allowed to float free from the rest of us; where a generation of young people are growing up without work, without prospects, without hope. None harder hit than the black youngsters held back by an unemployment rate approaching 50%." [1]

He said the riots had raised "alarming questions" about the country Britain had become, and he said David Cameron was "wrong" to brand the riots "criminality pure and simple". The unrest had served to expose "pernicious inequality", but also underlined the folly of Government policies, such as cutting youth services and withdrawing the education maintenance allowance for 16–19 year olds in secondary education. He said:

> "Rather than addressing the complex long-term factors that lie behind the alienation — the poverty, the lack of social mobility, young lives stunted by hope denied — they have instead reached for simplistic clichés about moral decay."[2]

The TUC leader's language reflected the same 'masters and slaves' division that characterised industrial relations in Britain back in the Industrial Revolution and in the days of the Combination Acts, the Tolpuddle Martyrs, the Chartist Movement, the beginnings of the Trades Unions and the Labour Movement. He lambasted the present Coalition Government's policies:

> "And yet, as they have retreated to Victorian language about the undeserving poor, they have said nothing about moral disintegration among the rich, the financiers with huge assets sneakily channelled through the tax havens, the out-of-control traders and speculators who razed our economy to the ground and the super-rich tax cheats whose greed impoverishes our schools and hospitals."[3]

11.2 Us and Them

This 'us and them' language has been a major factor in social relationships in Britain since the beginning of industrialisation and urbanisation in the eighteenth century. It is to be seen everywhere in Britain, even in relationships between north and south. Those in the south are popularly supposed to be allied to the ruling classes, and those of the north are reputedly the downtrodden workers. This divide can even be seen in patterns of voting whereby northern counties persistently vote Labour from one generation to the next, while the south identify more readily with the Conservatives or the Lib Dems.

Of course this is a caricature, but it has persisted for generations and is still here today, not only among older people. Young people who are currently suffering from high rates of unemployment and the increased difficulties of obtaining a university education in the austerity programmes resulting from the 2008 banking crisis[4] are likely to inherit the social class myths of the older generation. Ethnic minorities in inner-city areas have no difficulty in identifying with this rationale of the dispossessed. In Britain today there are more black young people in prison than in university, which reinforces the sense of injustice and inequality of the social system which is the daily experience of young black people in British cities.

Social class division has become institutionalised at all levels of British society since the early days of urbanisation and industrialisation in the eighteenth century, but over the past forty years it has increasingly extended into the black population. As a community of the oppressed, the second generation of West Indian migrants easily identified with their white co-belligerents as victims of the oppressors. The English inner-city working class descendants of white slavery, such as those represented in the rhetoric of Brendan Barber the TUC leader, reported above, found a common cause in their shared experience of daily life. Although neither of them knew the other's history, and each of them had little or no knowledge of their own history, the fact that they were thrown together in an urban ghetto of shared deprivation was sufficient to overcome differences of race and ethnic culture.

11.3 White Slavery

In sociological terms social class is only predicable of an industrial society, but in Britain the roots of social differentiation go back into the centuries of feudalism that pre-dated the Industrial Revolution. The roots of white slavery have already been noted in Chapter 8 in the struggle for workers' rights that began in the eighteenth century. But its institutionalisation within wider society took place during the Victorian era, by the end of which the largest sector in the workforce was employed in the service industry, and an 'upstairs, downstairs' stratification of society had become acceptable as being divinely ordered. The Victorians happily sang about this divine order in hymns such as *All things bright and beautiful*, which had the verse:

> *The rich man in his castle,*
> *The poor man at his gate,*
> *God made them high and lowly,*
> *And ordered their estate.*[5]

This was a case of religion being used to reinforce the socially acceptable stratification of society and to keep the poor and powerless in their place.

By the mid-nineteenth century, at the height of Victorian prosperity, the 'white slavery' which had begun in the factories, the textile mills and coalmines of eighteenth century England, was a characteristic much in evidence in the backstreet sweatshops of Dickensian London and other big cities. Sweated labour became a major social issue in the second half of the nineteenth century in many British cities, and especially in London, where living conditions in some areas were appalling. There were no state social workers but some of the most reliable first-hand reports come from missionaries employed by the London City Mission. An 1847 account reported:

As many as 20 persons sometimes live in one room, in addition to dogs, cats, and rabbits. The filth and stench of some of these rooms renders them hardly endurable.... Often the missionary has been overpowered, and obliged to retreat into New Oxford Street for air, and, although he has been but a few months in the district, his health has been more affected during that short time, than it had been for years previously; while the first missionary on the district lost his life through fever. [6]

One of the LCM missioners gave a first-hand account of his experience of visiting families in the London slums:

On my first appointment to the district, in 1845, I was called upon to encounter a severe trial. I was seized with violent itchings between the joints, accompanied with redness. I appeared to have caught the itch… Bugs and fleas, and other vermin … have tormented me sadly… Whilst visiting at night I have sometimes seen numbers of bugs coursing over my clothes and hat… The stenches have sometimes been so bad that I have been compelled to retreat.[7]

Reference has already been made to the forty-six year campaign to persuade Parliament to limit the number of hours a child could be made to work in a day.[8] The battles for simple justice in industrial practice, and the long struggle to improve living and working conditions for the poor, plus the hundred year long political fight to obtain universal suffrage, combined to leave a bitter taste in the mouths of working people that lasted right through the nineteenth century and lingered through most of the twentieth.

The strong social class-differentiated patterns of society were highly evident in the First World War in the differences between the officer class and the non-commissioned soldiers. These class differences carried over into the grim years of depression in the 1920s and well into the 1930s with the long marches of the unemployed. It was not until the threat of German rearmament under Hitler's Third Reich, which forced Britain onto a war footing with consequent full employment, that things began to change. The 1939–45 war was a great social leveller. But it was not until the post-World War II period of the Attlee Labour Government and the introduction of the Welfare State that serious efforts were made to tackle social class inequalities.

Legislation, however, can make provision for the poor, but it cannot change deeply embedded social attitudes, especially those that have become institutionalised into the fabric of society over many generations. Without such a change of social attitudes, welfare provision is likely to create a class of dependency with the expectation of rights without responsibilities. At root, this has been the basic failure of the Welfare State which was exposed in the violent inner-city disturbances of August 2011. Clearly, the disturbances were not rooted in economic deprivation or there would have been outbreaks in Glasgow and other cities where there are severe pockets of poverty. A search for the root causes of the Tottenham riots and their copycat related disturbances has to be directed elsewhere.

11.4 Social Injustice

There is strong sociological evidence to suggest that one of the major roots of the disturbances is to be found in an amalgam of two sources of social injustice. They are to be found in British 'colonial slavery' and in 'white slavery' in Britain. In this book we have been examining both these issues in their historical context. It remains to be proven that the legacies of both these social phenomena are still alive and socially significant. It is easy to trace the social class attitudes of present-day working class people in Britain back to the eighteenth, nineteenth and early twentieth century struggles for justice. It is, however, much less recognised in the general population that there is a particular legacy of slavery among black communities in Britain whose roots are in the British West Indies. The statistical evidence for this was clearly demonstrated in 2007 in the questionnaires completed by visitors to the *Zong* slave ship (as described in Chapter 7), revealing that only 9% of the white British people who visited the slave ship claimed to know a lot about colonial slavery. These were people who were sufficiently interested in the subject to visit the slave ship and pay to see an exhibition, so it would be reasonable to conclude that an even smaller percentage of the general population have any significant knowledge of the slave trade and the three hundred years of slavery in the West Indies under British rule. Yet it was this period that moulded the social heritage of the African-Caribbeans who form a significant part of the inner-city population of many of our major British cities. Clearly, most British people are quite unaware of the background and history of migrants who have settled among them.

The *Zong* research showed that African-Caribbeans, while lacking detailed knowledge of colonial slavery, had significantly greater awareness of the Atlantic slave trade than either white British or Africans. The Africans in Britain proudly say that they have never been slaves. But it was African princes who sold their countrymen to the white traders. The survey showed that 62% of Caribbeans had heard of the Atlantic slave trade, in contrast to only 37% of white British and 46% of Africans. This is despite the fact that in the Caribbean most people do not want to talk about colonial slavery. They are certainly aware of it, but they have not allowed a root of bitterness to overwhelm their national psyche and destroy their natural good humour.

11.5 Colonial Slavery

Until 2007, and the 200th anniversary of the abolition of the slave trade, the subject of colonial slavery was not generally taught in British schools. It is still absent from many history books. This 200-year silence has created an enormous gap in the knowledge of British people of the history and social background of the African-Caribbeans who live and work among them in most UK cities. It is therefore necessary to take a further look at the process of social assimilation that has taken place since the arrival of the *Empire Windrush,* bringing the first batch of immigrants from the West Indies in 1948. As far back as 1963, in a study published by Oxford University Press for the London Institute of Race Relations, I was warning of the consequences of a lack of any cohesive policy of social integration for the newcomers. I said:

> There is abundant evidence to show that the West Indian minority is not being absorbed into the community. The dream of Britain being able to produce a multiracial society at the very centre and heart of a great multiracial Commonwealth is fast fading into the realm of unattainable ideals.[9]

At that time I was slowly moving away from the ideal of full integration and Britain being open to all citizens of the Commonwealth. As already stated,[10] I had opposed the terms of the Commonwealth Immigrants Act 1962, which reinforced the popular view that immigrants were 'a problem' whose numbers must be restricted. At that time I was becoming aware of the extent to which I had absorbed attitudes of patronage as part of my white heritage. As I absorbed the experience of travelling in the West Indian islands and applied it to the situation in Britain, I began to see the wider implications of an unfolding tragedy on an immense scale in our inner-city areas.

At that time there was already a small emerging middle class in the migrant communities who had achieved a sufficient level of education to enable them to enter the professions. Conversations with them in the mid-1960s helped me to recognise the wider realities of the social situation that was developing around me in Tottenham. One of those who influenced my thinking was a young West Indian social worker whose testimony I published in a symposium to which he made a valuable contribution. He spoke of the way in which the British had de-Africanised the whole of the slave population, and he himself had been brought up in an education system that institutionalised this. He said:

> It was in the field of education that Anglicising was most evident. What young Jamaican did not sing lustily 'Rule Britannia', or recite 'Children of the Empire'? Who were the heroes of Jamaican children? Not Paul Vogel, William Gordon; but Nelson, Rodney, Clive of India and Gordon of Khartoum. The British poets were our poets. The British Schools Examinations were our examinations; the schools in Jamaica were in so many instances run on identical lines and had similar curricula to those in England. Thus, there were never any difficulties in transferring from one to the other. Yet some English people today are still amazed to know that Jamaicans' mother tongue is English![11]

11.6 Immigration

I was well aware of the shock experienced by migrants from the Caribbean when they entered Britain, and I have referred already to their expectations of a warm welcome on 'coming home' to the mother of the Commonwealth being shattered within the first few days, when they not only experienced the difficulties of finding accommodation and employment, but felt themselves to be unwelcome strangers in a strange land, even when they went to church. I personally became absorbed in living and working among members of the migrant community in the early days of the migration from the West Indies, and I internalised their problems. I fought battles on their behalf at both local and national level.

Membership of the Commonwealth Immigrants Committee

gave me access to members of the Government. I wrote extensively, did a weekly broadcast to the Caribbean on the BBC Overseas Service, and took part in numerous radio and television programmes through the 1960s. I was strongly influenced by a philosophical ideal of Commonwealth, which later I came to recognise was a form of paternalism or even a mild form of racism, which was a hangover from the days of Empire and white superiority.

In a penetrating comment on the opposition to the Commonwealth Immigrants Act of 1962, Elspeth Huxley wrote:

> Most people on the idealistic wing of our society opposed this Act on grounds of principle. Our long tradition of free entry by any citizens of the Commonwealth must not (they said) be broken; we are the heart and centre of the Commonwealth and must not deny to anyone its open shores. Here crops up, again, the image of the mother who has sent forth her sons and mustn't slam the door in the face of any who want to come home. This is, alas, at bottom, an imperialist, paternalistic notion, and it's ironical that the most anti-imperialist of our thinkers should be the ones to voice it most emphatically. Broken and tarnished lies the mother image; Asians and Africans never were her sons; anyway, her dugs are dry.[12]

11.7 Social Darwinism

The danger of hanging onto this image of past Empire lies in the paternalism and elements of racism, strands of which were present in the abolitionist campaign of the late eighteenth and early nineteenth centuries. Anthropological theories played a part in the debates, where abolitionists espoused a monogenic theory, which maintained that all mankind was descended from a single origin. The pro-slavery propagandists, both in Britain and America, drew upon the theory of polygenesis maintaining that the discovery of new peoples and new cultures gave credence to the belief that the different races came from separate origins. All this was blown apart in 1859, when Darwin published his *Origin of Species*. But it was not long before there emerged a kind of 'Social Darwinism', of whose propagandists Sheila Paterson wrote:

> They attempted to translate Darwin's doctrines into a law of social development. Stronger nations tended to prevail over others and stronger nations tended to be better. This led to an association of the ideas of nation and race, an affirmation of the innate superiority of the Aryan, Nordic and Teutonic races, and the assumption of a socio–cultural hierarchy of races.[13]

It was a form of Social Darwinism that lay at the heart of Adolf Hitler's Third Reich and its concept of racial superiority that led to the central European Holocaust. Although Nazism was defeated in 1945, its racist ideology has lingered on in fringe pseudo-political groups across Europe, with their irrational prejudice and xenophobic hatred. In 1960s Britain, as we have seen, traces of this xenophobia were quite widespread where black immigrants were settling.

11.8 Racism

When my house was attacked in 1963 by members of a far right racist group who painted the words 'NIGGER LOVER'[14] on the pavement in front of the house, the resultant press reports brought a sack load of abusive letters. A typical comment about the immigrants was 'They're no more British than the man in the moon; and they never will be!' Many of the letters were anonymous; clearly the writers did not wish to be identified, although at that time there was nothing in law to prevent them making insulting and racist comments. In fact it took the nation another forty-three years before such abuse was legally banned by the Racial and Religious Hatred Act 2006.

The West Indian social worker to whom reference has already been made had originally believed that this kind of racial hatred was confined to small groups of extremists who, he believed, could not be representative of Britain, which he believed to be a Christian country. He wrote about his personal expectation on arrival in Britain:

> The majority will be kind and welcoming regardless of troubles caused by a minority. Beside this view, we can place the idea of British justice being there. 'Innocent until proven guilty' means a reasonable chance to gain admittance to the new society. These notions of fair play in a Christian society may not be accessible in the same way that job prospects are, but they are strongly believed by West Indians and disillusionment in this respect has a disturbing effect upon the whole of life for an immigrant. Of course, the Jamaican while still accepting that these principles guide official institutions like the Courts and the Church, has to contend with the general public, and it is here he finds his real proving ground.[15]

But the bitterest disappointment came in their treatment at the hands of officials and the police. Far from 'innocent until proven guilty' being a reality, their daily experience was the reverse. In the 1960s and 1970s in many inner-city areas the police operated a system of stopping people on suspicion of either having committed a crime or being prepared to be involved in crime (colloquially known as the 'sus laws'). This led to many people from the immigrant communities being stopped and searched, and if they objected it led to arrest. Many times I have been to the police station in response to a call from an anxious relative of someone claiming to be wrongfully arrested, and after listening to the evidence I have succeeded in getting a release.

Many times I have been told by policemen that if they saw

a black man running they would automatically arrest him because he must be involved in wrongdoing, and if they saw groups of black youths gathering on the street, they suspected them of breaking the law or preparing to do so. I have a 1964 newspaper cutting of a report of when I appeared in court in Tottenham on behalf of an African member of my church. The press report stated that in my evidence I had said:

'Mr B... is a high born well-educated man and because he is a law student he is able to defend himself. But there are many from humbler circumstances quite unable to do anything against police charges. Mr B..., who was assistant to the Chief Scout in Nigeria, and was presented to the Queen on her visit there in 1957, was charged with using insulting behaviour in St Ann's Road Tottenham and with assaulting PC C.. F.. He maintained that the officer deliberately bumped into him and said, "You silly ***** when are you going back to your own country?" He said that he was "grabbed" and taken to the police car and dragged into the station. His requests to see a solicitor, to phone the Nigerian High Commissioner, and his wife, were refused by the police. The officer said that he was pushed and punched by Mr B.. The case was dismissed for insufficient evidence.'[16]

11.9 Police Injustice

In July 1968 the West Indian Standing Conference – London Region, issued a statement to its members saying that the Conference Secretary, Mr Geoff Crawford, had been approached by a BBC television producer asking for help in making a programme on relationships between the police and the black community. On 19 July 1968 Mr Crawford was informed by the BBC that the programme would be transmitted on *Cause for Concern* on 26 July and he was invited to take part in a ten minute live discussion to follow the film; the police were similarly invited.

Mr Crawford and the police saw a preview of the film

on 24 July, following which the police refused to take part in the discussion, saying that the programme was 'unfair, unobjective, grossly distorted, highly defamatory of individual police officers and libellous in four instances.'

Following a protracted argument the following day, the police threatened to stop the programme by issuing a High Court injunction. The BBC refused to withdraw the programme so the police threatened to prosecute the BBC and persons taking part in the film under Section 6 of the Race Relations Act (relating to the incitement to racial hatred). It was not until 26 July, the date when the programme was due for transmission, that the BBC finally gave way to police pressure and scrapped the programme.

The West Indian Standing Conference retaliated by issuing a notice to all their supporters:

In view of the police behaviour and tactics used to force the BBC to cancel this programme, Conference has decided to cease 'liaison' with the police and shall instruct its affiliated groups, and request other organisations, to do the same. Conference believes that all past efforts have been negated by this kind of behaviour. Conference also believes that the police do not intend to treat black people fairly and impartially. 'Liaison' on the part of the police was simply to whitewash and to hoodwink the community, especially the black community into believing that the British police are the fairest in the world.... The threat of possible action by the police, which in our view was a bluff, silences all discussion on the real and most explosive area in the field of race relations. Conference demands in the interest of harmonious community relations that the truth be told and appropriate action taken to ameliorate the police injustice and brutality against black people. The attitudes of the victims of police misconduct are hardening and so are the attitudes of some police officers. To withhold the truth from the public is to collaborate with the police and thus assist in the exacerbation of this problem.[17]

This complaint about police injustice was not given any publicity. Not a single British newspaper picked it up, and neither the BBC radio or television news, nor ITN dared to touch it. It was impossible to discover what had happened behind the scenes to cause a complete media blackout of this incident. There certainly must have been a very high level of interference, probably invoking 'security of the realm' legislation. But such incidents were not new. I myself had been building up a dossier of evidence over a number of years, which went on well into the 1970s. It was all part of the West Indian experience of discrimination.

11.10 Discrimination

Back in April 1967, the West Indian Standing Conference had complained to London Transport Board at their failure to promote any West Indian to the post of bus inspector. In their statement, the Conference said that they had been bringing this matter to the attention of London Transport Board for the past twelve years and they suspected that the Board was giving way to pressure from the Transport and General Workers Union, some of whose members refused to work under a black bus inspector. It was ironic that those who believed in the universal brotherhood of working men took a long time to recognise the equality of black workers. It was small wonder that West Indian first-generation immigrants had a strong sense of rejection, which affected all their social relationships.

That experience of discrimination which was there in 1967 is still strong today among members of the West Indian community. I was one of the speakers at a conference organised by the Mayor of London in City Hall in August 2007. It was part of the London commemorations of the 200th anniversary of the Abolition of the Slave Trade in 1807. The conference, hosted by Ken Livingstone, who was then London's Mayor, was attended by three hundred leaders from the black communities in Greater London. They came mostly from the West Indian communities. My contribution was to speak about Wilberforce and the abolition movement in Britain.

11.11 Ongoing Injustice

Dr Anthony Reddie[18] spoke on the theme 'The Untold Story of African Resistance'. He spoke about the way in which the resistance of the Africans themselves had been underplayed in the historical accounts by white historians, which has led to the continuation of the paternalistic attitudes of white middle-class professionals and the continuation of the demeaning of black people, which is part of the legacy of slavery today. At one point in his speech he said, "There are just sufficient black people in top positions in Britain today to convince the white population that the system is working." This statement brought thunderous applause from the black leaders who clearly fully supported his analysis of the present situation in British race relations.

A month earlier I had been invited to speak to the annual conference of the Association of Black Clergy, which brought together ordained ministers from several denominations, including the Church of England, Baptist and United Reformed Churches. During the conference I asked them about their own personal experience in community relationships. They were unanimous in saying that they experience discrimination in church appointments. They all said that the only appointments they are offered are in black inner-city areas. They are never offered the plum appointments of churches in salubrious middle class suburban areas or provincial towns. They pointed out that at that time there were only two senior black clergy in the Church of England —the Dean of Manchester and the

Archbishop of York. I remembered their statements the following month when listening to Anthony Reddie, so it was not surprising that this statement was so strongly applauded and affirmed by black leaders, most of whom came from what may be described as the emerging middle class in the migrant communities.

Earlier, in the autumn of 2006, during the preparations for the commemoration of the 200th anniversary of the abolition of the slave trade, black and white community leaders across London were invited to a private showing of the film 'Amazing Grace' which was due to be released the following year. Walden Media, who were promoting the film, said that they wanted frank comments from community leaders before the final cut of the film was made. I had recently published a book, *The Wilberforce Connection*,[19] for which I had done a considerable amount of research, and I noticed a number of historical inaccuracies in the film but it was clearly too late to change anything of substance.

The black leaders were very unhappy with the preview presentation which they said did not do justice to the level of black involvement in the abolition movement. They were also particularly upset at the triumphalist ending with a brass band of the Scots Guards playing 'Amazing Grace', which they said gave the impression that the battle for equality had been won and there was nothing further to be done. Nobody appeared to recognise that slavery is still very much alive in the world and that there is an ongoing legacy among former slaves that is as yet unresolved. The views of the black leaders were made known to Walden Media but no changes were made to the film. This added one more cause of resentment among black leaders that their views just do not count in a white dominated society, especially where there are big financial profits involved. The film's appeal to white society was clearly of much greater importance than historical accuracy! What was of great significance to the black community was simply entertainment to white people. It was another example of the marginalisation of the powerless.

11.12 The Churches

This lack of understanding in the general public that is still here today and was openly displayed in the 1950s and 1960s was also to be seen in churches of all denominations in that period. It is therefore also not surprising that the churches were no more successful in integrating black people than the secular institutions in Britain. The figures for church attendance recorded in Chapter 4 [20] showed that despite 69% of the population being in regular church attendance in the West Indies, only 4% of immigrants were attending London churches *of the same denomination.* In 1962 my visits to the West Indies had been sponsored by the British Council of Churches with the object of creating links between churches in the Caribbean with similar churches in the UK so that names of migrating churchgoers could be passed on.

There were, of course, enormous difficulties in operating such a scheme due to the high mobility of the migrants and their problems of finding suitable accommodation. Despite this, I contacted churches in every borough of Greater London, but there was a notable lack of interest so there was very little fruit from this endeavour. There was no warm welcome for the newcomers in most of the London churches. In my experience, very few clergy and nonconformist ministers went out of their way to help the migrants in their time of need. They were simply left to their own devices, which contributed to their disillusionment and their personal loss of faith. It has to be said that if the British churches had acted differently, and welcomed this huge influx of practising Christians from the Caribbean, the whole situation in our inner-city areas could have been transformed, and we would not be in the situation such as we have today.

It nevertheless needs to be recorded that from 1960 the growth of black-led Pentecostal churches was extremely rapid. The New Testament Church of God, which began in 1953, affiliated to the Church of God, Cleveland Tennessee, was one of the oldest of these churches in Britain. It made modest gains in its first six years, but then from 1960 their congregations throughout the country expanded exponentially. I reported this in a paper, read to sociology lecturers at Senate House in London University, where I linked their growth to the experience of 'relative deprivation'. I said that deprivation is not necessarily linked with economic factors.

Certainly the great majority of West Indians in Britain are not suffering from economic deprivation. Economically, they are far better off than they were in their homelands, but they are experiencing both ethnic and status deprivation. I have many times heard West Indians say that they had never thought of themselves as being 'coloured' until they came to Britain. Because of his colour (regardless of whether he is light-skinned or dark) the West Indian is forced into a peculiar status group that has all the characteristics of immobility common to a caste.[21]

11.13 First Generation

This relative deprivation was the major reason why migrants who had been regular church attenders in the Caribbean did not feel comfortable in similar denominational churches in Britain, but turned instead to the black-led congregations. The British churches in these areas were largely middle class institutions, although they attracted respectable working class people in their congregations. The lay leadership was usually drawn from middle class members. By contrast, churches in the West Indies do enjoy the widespread support of the working classes, especially in the rural areas from which the majority of the first generation of migrants came. When they went to church in Britain they experienced a sense of social distance in comparison with their middle class, socially secure, white fellow-worshippers. This increased their unease and reinforced their belief that they were not welcome. Even those from Pentecostal backgrounds did not feel at ease in English Pentecostal assemblies. The black-led churches rapidly became a meeting ground for expatriates, where they could relax and not have to speak formal English.

The sermons in these churches often reflected the daily life experience of the migrants in Britain. They were usually biblically-based exhortations dealing with the wickedness of the world, the sufferings of the people of God, the coming great day of deliverance, the future judgement and suffering of evildoers, and the final vindication and joy of the faithful. There was a strong eschatological element present in the teaching given to church members of the New Testament Church of God which was present in a New Year message from their National Overseer, published in December 1969. After dwelling upon the wickedness of the world in which he bracketed drug addicts and murderers with demonstrators and wildcat strikers, he wrote:

Because of these things men's hearts are filled with fear and they are determined to leave this earth, in some form or the other, without hope of eternal life. However, we the children of God have a blessed hope that Jesus is coming again. We shall be leaving this sin-cursed earth with him, when he returns in midair for his bride, won't that be a happy time! With this hope in view, we are labouring on in the great harvest field, toiling on, and let us not faint for we know our labour will not be in vain in the Lord, for in due season we will reap if we faint not. Hence we keep at it, working in all circumstances for the Master, denying ourselves and taking up his cross to follow him.

Our objective is to promote the cause of Christ, and to build up his kingdom, by all means trying to save some.[22]

11.14 Second Generation

This type of message accorded well with the life experience of first-generation immigrants but it had no relevance to young people in the second generation. Children were brought to church with adults in the 1960s and 1970s, but once they approached teenage years difficulties mounted. These young people were born in Britain and educated with their local white peer group. They were keen to find acceptance and soon realised that church attendance, far from helping integration, added social distance and increased the difficulty of establishing and maintaining social acceptance. This second generation largely grew away from the church and adopted the mores of their friends and neighbours in the host society, including patterns of family breakdown and single parenthood.

This second generation, particularly those born in the 1970s and 1980s are now the parents of the third generation —some of whom were involved in the riots. They are fully adjusted to life in the ghettos of urban deprivation, drugs and despair, which is the only environment they have known. But in sociological theory the third generation in a migrant community will react in one of two ways.[23] If they are socially secure, as is the common experience in the USA in the case of white immigrants of European extraction, and the Polish immigrants in the UK, they will then seek to emphasise their distinctiveness by searching for their roots. If they do not have that security it usually results in an increase in anomie, which may give rise to hopelessness and despair, or to antisocial ideologies and aggressive actions.

In the case of the British West Indians, they have neither the family stability nor the strong cultural connections to enable them to search for their roots. Their African roots were entirely destroyed by colonial slavery. They lost their tribe, their family, their African name, their culture, their language and their ancestral heritage. They were branded with the mark of the plantation and given the name of the plantation owner. As already noted, many still see their English surname as the branding of slavery. So today they are unable to explore their roots for a distinctive culture of which they can be proud. Their dysfunctional family life and their personal insecurity are further driving forces towards social alienation which make them increasingly vulnerable to the drive to seek refuge in local gang life.[24]

11.15 Third Generation

Many of these third-generation children have never known the mentoring of a father or received strong educational encouragement and support. From an early age they are the target of drug dealers who offer them money to deliver a package in the next street. Once they do this they come under the power of the dealer and are soon sucked into the network. They are proud when they are asked to look after a gun which they hide in their bedroom. They are drawn into a gang for their own protection, which has strict rules of conformity. The gang is a substitute family, which gives identity, status, respect and security, but the one thing the gang cannot do is to give love, encouragement and hope.

Many of the gangs are mixed colour because race is no longer a valid social division. What has taken place under the impact of shared deprivation is an amalgam of socio-cultural values drawn from a fusion of the heritage of white slavery and colonial slavery. Both black and white young people have been forced into a common mould by a shared experience of relative deprivation in an aggressively acquisitive culture where celebrities are highly valued and style and material wealth are worshipped.

The 'masters and slaves' mindset of both white and black young people moulds their outlook on life. It is an explosive mixture, a time bomb with a short fuse. Once it is triggered, the pent-up rage of the urban slaves against the masters, the ruling classes, the owners of wealth and property and the symbols of their oppression, suddenly explode. The fashion goods and material things which, in their view, should rightly be theirs, but have been unjustly denied to them, are uniquely available for the taking. The chaos of the riot is the opportunity for acquisition as well as the joy of hurting the oppressors. The unspoken sentiment of many in the ghettos is: Roll on the next riot! Bring it on!

Notes

[1] TUC Conference 2011: quoted from the TUC website September 2011.

[2] *Ibid.*

[3] *Ibid.*

[4] Student admissions for the year 2012/13 were reported to be 54,000 less than the previous year.

[5] This verse from 'All things bright and beautiful' was dropped from most hymn books by the second half of the twentieth century.

[6] The London City Mission Annual Report 1847, quoted in Donald M Lewis, *Lighten Their Darkness: The Evangelical Mission to Working-Class London 1828 – 1860*, Paternoster Press, London, 2001, p. 165.

[7] Quoted in Clifford Hill, *The Wilberforce Connection,* Monarch Books, London, 2004, p. 227.

[8] See chapter 8.

[9] Clifford Hill, *West Indian Migrants and the London Churches*, Oxford University Press, London, 1963, p. 77.

[10] Chapter 6, section 6.4.

[11] A West Indian Social Worker; in Clifford Hill and David Matthews, *Race: a Christian Symposium, Gollancz*, London, 1968, pp. 158–9.

[12] Elspeth Huxley, *Back Street New World – A Look at Immigrants in Britain*, Chatto and Windus, London, 1964, pp. 152–153.

[13] Sheila Paterson, *Racial Images and Attitudes in Britain – The Background*, in Clifford Hill and David Matthews, *op. cit.*, pp. 63–64.

[14] Chapter 4, section 4.5.

[15] *Ibid.*, p. 162.

[16] *The Tottenham Herald*, 2 October 1964.

[17] Issued by Lewis Chase, public relations officer WISC, London, July 1968. This paper is part of a collection of papers in my personal library.

[18] Dr Anthony Reddie spoke as Research Fellow in Black Theological Studies for the Methodist Church and the Queens Foundation for Ecumenical Theological Education.

[19] Clifford Hill, *The Wilberforce Connection*, Monarch, London, 2004.

[20] Chapter 4, section 4.7.

[21] Unpublished record of speech made.

[22] Oliver Lyseight, *Newsie*, New Testament Church of God, Birmingham, December 1969.

[23] See the chapter on the Third Generation Theory, section 5.4.

[24] Reported in *The Times*, 13 September 2011.

Chapter Twelve

FUTURE HOPE

Throughout the foregoing chapters of this book the objective has been to convey a valid historical and sociological analysis of the background to the riots which swept through some inner-city areas of Britain in August 2011. This analysis throws light upon a range of complex social issues that affect other parts of the UK and may also have relevance for other nations in the Western world, particularly the USA, where similar social tensions exist. In this final chapter the intention is to draw some conclusions which necessarily take us outside the realm of academic sociology and its canons of 'value freedom'. These concepts are, however, based upon many years of research and personal involvement in inner-city community life.

12.1 Legacy of Slavery

We have identified what can best be described as a 'mindset of slavery' that exists in many individuals and affects whole communities in inner-city areas. This is not an easy concept to define. The Oxford English Dictionary defines a 'slave' as 'a person who is the legal property of another or others and is bound to absolute obedience'. The mindset of slavery is where a person has no alternative other than to accept a social position of inferiority and servitude. It is usually accompanied by a sense of injustice which may be either rationalised or suppressed. It is in contrast to the spirit of 'servanthood' whereby a person willingly undertakes to serve or to care for others.

The contrast between slavery and servanthood is extremely important for understanding the social situation of inner-city areas of Britain which are characterised by a mixture of African, African-Caribbean and native white British people, all of whom have a common faith basis in Christianity which provided the foundation of their social values. At his last meal with his disciples, Jesus gave them a practical example of 'servanthood' by kneeling and washing their feet, a task usually performed by a slave in a rich man's household.[1] He was turning upside down the social conventions of his day by voluntarily serving those who were in an inferior social position.

A modern example of 'servanthood' was seen at the 2012 London Olympic Games when G4S had failed to produce the paid officials to provide a service to the visitors. Hundreds of men and women from all over the country volunteered their services as 'Games Makers'. The cheerful 'nothing is too much trouble' spirit in which they gave their services was a remarkable feature of the whole event which left an outstanding impression upon overseas visitors. They were from all strands of society and worked together serving the public with no expectation of reward other than the joy of serving and the satisfaction of knowing that they were participating in an event of national significance in which their contribution was much needed.

The long struggle for justice which we have traced from the Industrial Revolution through to the first half of the twentieth century was the formative period for the social differentiation in Britain which needs to be broken. It was the womb out of which were born our present-day social class attitudes. If we were to produce a scale of social class attitudes, at one end of the continuum would be the attitudes of the traditional aristocracy with their ascribed positions of social privilege, and at the other end would be inner-city people who are born into what is basically a 'social caste system' lacking any form of social status, from which there is little or no escape. It is amongst the latter that we have identified a mindset of slavery whereby they accept an ascribed social position as being 'outside mainstream society' and where there is no possibility of social mobility. They tend therefore to live by a system of in-group norms, derived from identifying with the local community, and in some instances provided by a local gang.

The common denominator between workers in the Industrial Revolution and workers in colonial plantation slavery was the division between their position and that of the 'masters' who had a monopoly of social and political power. In both cases the social position of powerlessness and inferiority became deeply embedded in the personality of the workers who were born into a 'social caste system' from which there was no escape. They accepted their social position as inevitable, although not necessarily willingly.

What we are describing as a 'mindset of slavery' became institutionalised in Dickensian Britain and is well depicted in the Victorian drama 'Upstairs Downstairs', and in the early twentieth century 'Downton Abbey' society in which people accepted their social positions as being predetermined. The social inferiority of workers was unquestioned by the majority and this had a controlling effect upon their behaviour. It became deeply embedded in the personality and social genes of many working class communities that can still be seen in Britain today. This has strong similarities with the mindset of slavery that exists among some of the descendants of colonial slavery from the Caribbean, and the two have combined to produce a community of the oppressed in some inner-city areas of twenty-first century Britain.

This mindset of slavery produces an 'us and them' attitude — a sense of 'victimhood', of being a casualty of circumstances beyond their personal control, which may lead in one of two directions. We have described the theory of this social phenomenon in Chapter 5.[2] It may lead to positive endeavours to overcome social obstacles, as in the case of those who have achieved professional status such as David Lammy MP, or to the internalisation of problems and low self-esteem, which may lead to depression, self-loathing and self-harm, and even under certain circumstances to suicide, the ultimate self-harm. Or it may lead to anti-social activities, petty criminal behaviour, or membership of a sub-cultural group with its own set of in-group social values which are at variance with the values of wider society. This is typical of the many gangs in inner-city areas that are territorially based, with each defending their own 'turf' and providing identity and 'belongingness' to youths from dysfunctional families. The major question with which we are concerned in this chapter is not so much the existence of such a mindset of slavery, for which there is overwhelming evidence, but how it can be overcome.

12.2 Caribbean Character

We have already looked at the historical background and the sufferings of workers in the factories and mines of eighteenth century Britain and on the sugar plantations of the West Indies. We have not, however, mentioned the colonial emancipation which, far from setting the Africans free from the mindset of slavery, actually reinforced and institutionalised it.

In 1833 slavery was declared illegal throughout the British Empire but there was a five year period in which the emancipation was supposed to be completed. In the final stage, as we have noted, in 1838, it was the slave *owners* who were compensated, *not the slaves*. £20 million of British taxpayers' money was given in compensation to the plantation owners for the loss of their 'property'. But nothing was given to the Africans who had been torn from their native communities, transported 3,000 miles across the Atlantic and forced into servitude through 300 years of colonial rule. Not a penny was paid to the emancipated slaves, the victims of injustice! The redemption price was paid to the *oppressors*, *not to the oppressed*. This injustice in the 1833 Abolition of Slavery Act has left an indelible stain upon British colonial history. The emancipation actually followed the same character of injustice as the enslavement. It reinforced and institutionalised the social standing of the Africans as inferior beings.

It is, however, possible to trace a quite remarkable outcome which history has never acknowledged, although it has been hugely influential in determining the social character of the people of the Caribbean islands. In the years leading up to the emancipation there was great fear among members of the white population that there would be a bloodbath once the slaves were set free. That same fear was present when I visited Jamaica in 1962, in the run-up to the proclamation of Independence in August that year. But there was no violent revolution on either occasion. Instead, the people gave thanks to God for their freedom, and set about building new lives for themselves and their children.

12.3 Nation–building

This is not the place to trace the history of the former colonies in the West Indies, but it is relevant to note the amazing act of nation-building in Jamaica that has taken place in a relatively short space of time. Instead of bemoaning the injustice they suffered, the people set to work with a will to transform their environment, to build a new social life as free people, and to establish a prosperous economy, from which, increasingly, the majority of the population would benefit. Of course, there have been many social tensions and outbreaks of violence since the 1830s, just as there have been in Britain. But a great deal has been achieved in Jamaica with very little help from powerful Western nations.

Undoubtedly, the driving force behind this, in addition to their common African origins, was a shared vision of a free society and a shared belief system which produced their own version of a work ethic and shared social values. The driving force behind this unique ethic of society was Christianity, which had been brought to the West Indies by courageous missionaries during the period of colonial slavery. Many of them suffered severe persecution and even murder at the hands of the planters and colonial rulers who were afraid that by giving the people the teaching of Jesus which turned upside-down the values of the world, it would encourage the slaves to demand their freedom. This fear grew in the early nineteenth century as some fiery preachers arose in the slave communities, notably Samuel Sharpe, the leader of the Baptist church in Montego Bay, who was hanged in 1832 by the colonial government with more than three hundred other African slaves, just one year before the Abolition of Slavery Act that set them free.

Following emancipation, the Christian faith spread rapidly and became indigenised, with local home-grown pastors and preachers serving local congregations who took over from the missionaries. When I visited Barbados, Trinidad and Jamaica, I travelled the length and breadth of Jamaica, talking with community leaders in remote villages, as well as urban and suburban groups and families. I was tremendously impressed with the character and resilience of the people, although I noticed that the larger and more prestigious churches were still being led by British missionaries.

As recorded in Chapter 3,[3] I had fully expected to meet with resentment at the injustice they had suffered at the hands of my British forebears. It was only some 120 years after the emancipation. The grandparents of the older people I met had known slavery. But, far from a cold, hostile attitude, I was met with warmth and generosity everywhere except in the ganja–smoking Rasta community in West Kingston, some of whom were remnants of the former, warlike Maroons. But they were a tiny fraction of the nation, a small outlawed group who were by no means representative.

Of course, they were all aware of their history. This was the remarkable thing! They knew about the slavery suffered by former generations — but that was in the past, it was not forgotten, but *it was forgiven*. Everywhere I went, I met with people who knew the Bible and its teaching that God loves us and forgives our sins. They regularly prayed the prayer that Jesus had taught his disciples "*Forgive us our sins **as we forgive others** who sin against us*."[4] They knew the teaching of the Bible that when God forgives us he doesn't harbour resentment and keep on raking up our past offences to throw in our faces at opportune moments like we human beings so often do to each other. The Apostle Paul once defined true love in a letter to the people in Corinth, saying, '*Love is not self-seeking, it is not easily angered, **it keeps no record of wrongs**.*'[5]

This *keeping no record of wrongs* which is one of the marks of true Christian faith was clearly something that most of the population in Jamaica had put into practice. I was told that 95% of the population of Jamaica at the time of my visit would have counted themselves as Christians and most of them were regular churchgoers. I had hundreds of conversations with people who demonstrated this kind of love in their lives and actually showed this kind of love towards me, a stranger, from the nation that had committed such unspeakable cruelty and injustice towards their forebears. This forgiveness and generosity is of enormous significance in understanding what happened to the first generation of migrants settling in Britain in the 1950s and 1960s.

12.4 Nelson Mandela

The peaceful transition of South Africa from a white dominated apartheid regime to a black majority democracy was largely due to the inspiration of one man, Nelson Mandela. South Africa could so easily have become a bloodbath as it was reaching the point where the black majority could no longer be held in subjection to the white minority. But for one man's 'Long Walk to Freedom' there could not have been a peaceful revolution because, as world history amply demonstrates, those who hold power never willingly relinquish that power. It either has to be forcefully taken from them or there has to be a more powerful ideology that persuades them that this is in their own best interest. Nelson Mandela provided that persuasion through his own personal example of forgiveness and reconciliation.

It is surely remarkable that any man can walk away from twenty-seven years of imprisonment that included hard labour and total subjection to his jailers and yet not display bitterness and the desire for revenge. He had already won the respect of his jailers and upon his release he set about following a policy of nation-building through mutual respect, forgiveness and reconciliation. This did not mean simply forgetting the past but actually facing the past injustices and oppression by the white minority, which required both truth and the active forgiveness of those who had suffered under apartheid so that black and white could move together into a new era as one nation.

Nelson Mandela's spirit of forgiveness was in strong contrast to that of Robert Mugabe, whose policy was to reverse the distribution of power in the former colony of Southern Rhodesia. His was a desire for revenge and inflicting upon the white population a regime of brutal oppression which has proved disastrous for both the economic and social health of Zimbabwe. The contrast between South Africa and Zimbabwe is a living demonstration of the power of love and forgiveness over that of hatred and revenge. It is Mandela's spirit of nation-building through the reconciliation of different cultures that is greatly needed in Britain today; but so too is the recognition of past injustices and the active seeking of forgiveness and reconciliation.

12.5 Tottenham

In 1962 at the end of my visit to the West Indies I returned to England and to the thousands of men and women from the West Indies whom I had come to know in London, and to those who were part of my own church community in Tottenham. I came back with a new respect for the immigrants and a greater understanding of their character. It was at this point that many of the attitudes of British professional-class 'paternalism' dropped away from me. I began to make deeper friendships on the basis of equality and appreciation of the character and qualities of the settlers.

But more importantly, I began to understand this first generation of migrants and to see them in a new light. Back in Jamaica they felt proud to be British as they identified with everything British and they saw British history, which they learned in school, as their own. This was 120 years after the end of slavery yet the children of this British colony were still being robbed of their African identity and taught about the kings and queens of England as though this was their heritage. This Anglicisation of Caribbean culture was reinforced by the presentation of the Christian gospel which had come from Britain, and many of the churches in the towns and villages of Jamaica were still served by ministers from Britain: a living demonstration of ecclesiastical paternalism!

The brainwashing of Caribbeans before emigration to Britain convinced them that they would be coming to a land of paradise, a nation of Bible-believing Christians to which they themselves would easily relate as part of the family. To come to Britain was the height of their ambition, the fulfilment of a dream — they would be 'going home' and they were sure that a warm welcome awaited them, matching the warmth in their hearts for their British brothers and sisters. The cold British winter was unimaginable in the tropical heat of the Caribbean, but the physical shock of snow and ice was as nothing compared with the bitter social and spiritual experience that awaited them.

12.6 Betrayed

It was just unbelievable to discover that all the British were not in church on Sundays and that they did not practise the love and generosity that they preached. The first generation of West Indian migrants were utterly disillusioned and many were quite broken-hearted. They felt deceived and betrayed. Everything they had believed about their 'homeland', centre of the great British Empire and head of the Commonwealth, was torn asunder by the reality of life in Britain. It was as though members of their own family, those whom they loved and trusted, had deceived them. All that they had been taught, the foundation of their hopes and dreams, was shattered. It was as though part of the life within them was suddenly aborted, ripped from the womb of their personality by those they held in high esteem. It tore their faith apart: even when they went to church, they were not welcome. Those who had taught them the faith had betrayed them.

12.7 Pentecostals

As already noted, the faith of Pentecostals actually survived the shock of migration better than Anglicans and Baptists and others, because they had been used to being regarded as 'different' in the West Indies. Although Pentecostal churches were few and far apart in England in the 1960s, they *did* expect to be accepted in the British Pentecostal assemblies, but even there they were not welcome, and those who had formerly held positions of responsibility as pastors and evangelists in the West Indies were not recognised as leaders in Britain. They felt the bitterness of rejection. It was not long before they began to form small assemblies of their own. They began meeting for prayer, worship and fellowship in their homes. The British black churches were born, but most were born in a vale of tears.

The first generation of Pentecostal pastors were men and women of enormous courage and faith. They lived incredibly self-sacrificial lives. They worked to earn a living to support themselves and their families, while at the same time pastoring a growing community of expatriate Christians who were struggling to cope with the pressures of living and working in rundown overcrowded unsavoury areas of British cities. They faced opposition, prejudice and hardship with great fortitude, often working long hours but still having time to support the people in their growing congregations. It was at this stage that the new Pentecostal churches began serving not just the small number of those who had been Pentecostals in the West Indies, but drawing those from other denominations who had not felt comfortable in English churches. An additional struggle, as their numbers increased, was to find somewhere to meet or to persuade some reluctant church to close their ears to the 'noisy worship' and allow them to use their church hall.

Church attendance in this first generation of migrants plummeted from around 70% (in Jamaica) to 4% (in London),[6] which represents not only a massive social change in a whole community but a multitude of personal tragedies and disillusionment. The whole migrant population effectively became a depressed community, stigmatised as second-class citizens. The loss of their faith in God, together with the loss of their faith in being British, had both psychological and sociological effects. It destroyed two of the pillars of personal stability that had been with them from childhood and which had been major influences in personal character formation as well as in social identity.

12.8 Resilience and Determination

Cross-cultural or inter-ethnic friendships were quite rare in the early days, which increased both individual and corporate isolation. In 1963 I was the adviser in the production of a television documentary on mixed race marriage which was produced by Eric Morley using 'camera verity' techniques. I scoured London for mixed black-and-white couples, which were quite rare in those days. Listening to their stories of the irrational prejudice and sometimes hatred that they encountered was often quite harrowing. This kind of prejudice, of course, had its effect upon the whole migrant community. But the combined effect of the personal struggle for survival and belonging to a depressed minority community brought out the best character traits in many of the migrants. Their personal resilience and determination to succeed strengthened their resolve to overcome the problems that surrounded them. Their success produced the new professional middle class of Caribbeans that we have in Britain today, which has grown out of the working class roots. It is this latter factor that is of great sociological significance and is a factor to which we must return when looking to the future.

Several things happened in the early days; most notably the newly-formed churches with West Indian leadership became the hub of the ethnic communities in inner-city areas. Secondly, as we have recorded, the stresses and strains of life in the immigrant communities led to a high level of relationship breakdown in family life. Marriage became the social fashion for a period throughout the 1950s and early 1960s, but as the rate of marriage breakdown increased the number of weddings fell rapidly in the 1970s and subsequently. The family patterns began to revert to the matriarchal system that had been left behind in the West Indies, but were also influenced by the changes taking place in native British society where family breakdown was increasing.

12.9 Children

We have also seen that the most important social effect of all these changes and stresses within the migrant communities was the effect upon children where the presence of stable, caring fatherhood in many families was unknown. These second-generation children were not immigrants. They were British-born residents with all the rights of citizenship enjoyed by their white peer group in what was euphemistically known in the 1950s and 1960s as the 'host community'. Yet the children were born into a confused world where their personal identities as well as their social position were both ill-defined. The tragedy was that their parents never understood them. How could they? They were fully occupied with the demands of sheer survival, coping with hardship, providing for their household and dealing with the traumas of culture change from life in rural Caribbean communities to inner-city London or Birmingham *et al* that had blown their world apart.

So the children of first-generation immigrants had to learn to deal with their own problems of culture clash with little help from their absentee fathers and overworked mothers. In accordance with 'Third Generation Theory', as second generation they sought to be fully accepted into the 'host society'.[7] They were taken to church, or house meetings, by their parents and were nurtured in the values brought from the Caribbean by their first generation parents. They were thus pulled by two contrasting cultures, neither of which understood the other. Many despised school and developed a drop-out culture, following the most radical of their inner-city rebellious white schoolmates.

12.10 Parents

This second generation are now adults. The world they face is very different from that faced by their parents, the first generation of migrants. This second generation have never had to tramp the streets of London and other big cities searching for accommodation. Neither have they had to face the overt racism that met their parents everywhere they went. In comparison with their parents they have an easy life, but their unstable childhood environment has left its mark. They do not share either the social or the personal values of their parents and neither are they motivated by the same work ethic.

The second generation are now the parents of the third generation —the young people who were involved in the August 2011 riots. Many of this generation of parents now have no control over their children; they take little or no interest in their education, and often take no personal responsibility for their children's social behaviour. They themselves are disillusioned. Their experience of life in

Britain has generated major social anomie. Their parents did not understand the stresses of the two worlds of culture into which they were born. Now, as young adults and parents of the third generation, the experience of many has developed into a sense of social detachment and despair which has both influenced their children and been communicated back to them from their children. It has been a two-way process of social alienation, leading to the widespread formation of dysfunctional families combining to form communities of the dispossessed.

It is all too easy to blame the environment or the economy, the lack of employment opportunities or a low standard of education and other social factors that could produce 'ghettos of deprivation'. However the root issues do not simply lie in the physical or social environment but also in the less tangible factors of social conditioning and personal values.

The issues, therefore, are as much in the inner self as in the inner-city. The solution does not lie simply in improving the physical environment by pouring resources in to create better buildings, better schools, plush housing, well-equipped youth centres and community facilities. Slum clearance in British cities has often proved that the physical structures can be changed but unless you change the mindset of the people the whole area will degenerate in a single generation. Too much of this kind of social policy has been seen in the East End of London where post-World War II reconstruction policy produced high-rise social housing which rapidly became social disasters. East Enders have vivid memories of Ronan Point and the surrounding enclaves of concrete where vast social problems were created by taking people from their little town house communities and stacking them up into the sky. Yet another radically new approach is needed if we are to eradicate conditions that led to the explosion of pent-up fury, frustration, envy and desire that fuelled the

August 2011 riots.

12.11 Changing Society

A great deal has been written about the inequalities in our society and measures that need to be taken to redistribute wealth. **Daniel Dorling**, in *Injustice*,[8] offers an exhaustive analysis of the roots of social inequality, elitism, exclusion, prejudice and greed. He says:

> A general malaise of despair has settled over the populations of the rich countries as elitism has strengthened, exclusion has grown, prejudice has been raised a level and greed has expanded. This is despair for the future, despair that was felt throughout what was seen as the best of economic times, the late 1990s boom, despair which is now very much more palpable since those times have ended.[9]

He acknowledges that there has to be a change of mind and a change of beliefs in order to achieve a change in society, but he confesses that he has no idea how this can be achieved. In fact, he warns his readers[10] early in the book:

> You should know now that the argument at the end of this book is that recognising the problem is the solution.

Surely this may not be a spur to action but a recipe for despair!

Owen Jones in *Chavs*[11] also speaks with eloquent passion about what he sees as the 'demonization of the working class' by the prosperous middle classes who control 'the establishment'. He says that social mobility does not work for the poor because even if middle and working class children go to the same school the middle class children will always come out on top. He quotes research by Nicola Woolcock for this assertion,[12] and further states that:

> Intelligent children from England's richest fifth are seven times more

likely to go to university than intelligent children from the poorest 40 percent.[13]

Jones then says that working class children are highly unlikely to earn more than their parents, because 'Britain's class system is like an invisible prison.' He says:

> The demonization of working-class people is a grimly rational way to justify an irrational system.... But this demonization has an even more pernicious agenda. A doctrine of personal responsibility is applied to a whole range of social problems affecting certain working-class communities — whether it be poverty, unemployment or crime. In Broken Britain, the victims have only themselves to blame.[14]

This practice of blaming the victims for their own unfortunate social circumstances was highlighted in October 2012 when a gang of men from Rochdale were sent to prison for sexually abusing underage girls. This abuse had been known to both the police and social services since 2003 when a report had been submitted to the Home Office. A social worker had noted in her report that a fourteen year-old girl who was being abused by the gang had 'made a lifestyle choice', and therefore there was no case to stop the abuse. The victim was blamed and not the abusers.

Owen Jones calls for an alliance of trade unions with user groups to defeat the middle class establishment, and he believes that the answer to Britain's problems of social inequality lie in tackling the 'lack of affordable housing and secure well–paid jobs.'[15] But this would appear to intensify class warfare rather than provide a solution.

His analysis of Britain's inner-city social problems brings him to a similar conclusion to that of most social commentators today, such as that expressed by **Professor Richard Wilkinson** and **Kate Pickett** in *The Spirit Level*,[16] that the fundamental need is for greater equality. They claim that their research shows that the more unequal society is, the more social problems it has, such as crime and poor health. But they leave the reader with no credible answers to the rebalancing of society in order to overcome inequality. To be fair, they are epidemiologists, not social planners.

Will Hutton, in his usual passionate style, has given us a comprehensive treatise in *Them and Us*.[17] But he too expends considerable passion on describing the inequalities of society. He exposes the inherent greed that drives Western capitalism and the shortcomings of politicians who promise to deal with the banking system but do no more than tinker around the edges because they dare not oppose the market.

But he too offers no policies of creative change apart from acknowledging that a new culture and a new spirit are required together with a commitment to 'fairness' in order to bring about change in society. There are few who would disagree with such a statement but they would surely be justified in asking how such a new culture and new spirit are going to be generated!

David Lammy, in his excellent review of the background to the Tottenham riots,[18] gets nearest to offering solutions to the problems that he highlights. Clearly he has an empathy with the local population of the area where he was born and which he now serves as their Member of Parliament. He goes beyond denouncing the free market and the loan sharks who exploit the poor, and he gets to the heart of the problem by calling for policies which will give 'ordinary people more power in the marketplace'. He rightly uses the word 'empowerment' as a key to transforming society. It is the experience of powerlessness that is the essence of the spirit of slavery, and it is only by giving people power over the institutions that control their social environment that their personal dignity will be restored and they will gain a sense of self-worth which will give them the incentive to contribute creatively to society for the common good.

The 'us and them' and 'masters and slaves' attitudes have become so institutionalised in the white working classes in British society over the past three hundred years that nothing less than fundamental alterations in the structure of society can change them. We will never break the social class attitudes among working people until they are given a stake in society such as earning shares in the companies where they work so that they have an interest in increasing productivity and they share in the profits of their own labours.

Perhaps it is time to take this a stage farther and think outside the box; to stop looking to banks to carry out radical self-regulation (which they never will do so long as their staff are enjoying their big bonus lifestyles), or politicians to introduce reforms that will change the structures of society (which they won't do because they are part of the privileged elite, and elites never willingly give up their power and privileges). So who will deal with the massive social inequalities that create powerlessness and enslave whole communities?

If we are to get to the root of the issues in our society it is surely time to recognise that in recent history we have seen all the revolutionary political policies tried, from fascist totalitarianism to National Socialism and Communism, and they don't work! When will we recognise that it is only changed human beings who are capable of really changing the social environment? But how can we change the mindset of people? How can the greedy become generous? How can the self-centred become unselfish? How can pessimists become optimists? If we had found the answers to these questions we would not need the multitude of social analyses that pour out of social foundations and research institutes. But maybe the answer is a lot simpler.

12.12 Changing Lives

My own experience of living for most of my working years in inner-city areas of London underlines the need to change mindsets, and gives some indication of how this can be done. I too have a great love for the people of Tottenham and similar places. I share David Lammy's admiration for their resilience and strong sense of community responsibility. I, too, detest the loan sharks and others who exploit the poor and powerless. I lived and worked and identified with the local community (and football team!) in Tottenham for ten years before moving into the East End to undertake an even greater challenge (not just supporting the Hammers!). Soon after we moved into East Ham, the little team with whom I worked took responsibility for a large Presbyterian Church that had just closed. It was just off the High Street near East Ham station. Its buildings were extensive although in a poor condition, but ideal for putting our 'community development' principles into action.[19] Monica, my wife, took charge of the project. She likes to say that this was because we were short of 'good staff'. But actually she did a brilliant job and laid foundations which would bear fruit over the next forty years.

We began by doing a house-to-house visitation of the area to assess needs. The two outstanding needs which we could easily meet were an after school club for 'latchkey kids' where both parents were at work, and a lunch club with afternoon activities for the elderly. It was not long before we responded to these and to requests for a youth club. We soon identified the most disruptive lads and appointed them to various positions of responsibility. They devised their own set of rules and enforced discipline far more severely than we would have done. They organised work nights when everyone joined in painting and decorating and carrying out repairs to the buildings. From that time we had no broken windows as none of the locals would dare to vandalise our property: in fact, it was no longer 'our' property — it was theirs. They had a strong sense of ownership. Although our buildings were scruffy and lacked the modern facilities of the purpose-built youth club run by the Council just up the road, on the nights when we were open the Council youth club was virtually empty — our old church hall was the place to be! Gradually the buildings and the facilities were improved but the most important thing was the changed lives of some of the most disruptive boys in the community.

On one occasion our youth club was invaded by a gang from Stratford who evidently had been offended by some of our community. They managed to switch off the lights at the mains and fighting broke out in the hall. When the knives came out I went in to try to sort things out, not knowing if I would come out alive, while one of the staff went to ring the police. Within a few minutes two or three squad cars came screaming down the high street and officers began dragging the lads out. I saw them take one of our young leaders and I followed him outside where he was spreadeagled across the bonnet of a police car. I am normally very respectful to anyone in a uniform but my indignation at this injustice gave me the boldness to shout at the officer, "You let him go! He's not one of the attackers. He's a good lad!"

My unexpected intervention must have startled the officer. He immediately released him and went back into the hall to find some other miscreant. I met the young man in the street the following day and he came as near as possible to thanking me. I knew he had a police record and I knew a bit of his family life. Probably no-one had ever spoken up for him before, and certainly no-one had ever trusted him with responsibility as we had done. This was the start of a new chapter in his life and he went on to become a respected leader in the community with a strong Christian faith.

The Trinity Centre in East Ham is now a model of community development in a multi-faith area. The Centre marked their fortieth anniversary in November 2012 with a grand celebration of cultural diversity within an amazing unity of community. Many members of the Newham Council were present, and so too was Stephen Timms MP who represents the area in Parliament. Each of the different ethnic groups contributed to the evening with something that represented their particular culture and commitment. There were of course numerous speeches with reminiscences of the early days and the journey that had brought them to this point.

The evening concluded with a community meal in which some three hundred people were served by the men of the Indian community. Monica and I were honoured as founders. The senior Muslim leader described how his father had brought him to Trinity when he was five years old. He said that there was nowhere else in Newham that allowed Muslims to meet. This had changed his view of Christians. All the ethnic leaders spoke, and the Hindu leader wrapped us in a shawl that he said had been blessed in his temple. This was the highest honour that they could confer. As Christians we were deeply moved and humbled, and we took the opportunity of speaking about the love of God through Jesus our Saviour which inspired and motivated us.

The Centre today is a hub for the local community, providing a safe place to meet, regardless of age or ethnic background. Each individual is respected and encouraged not only to engage in the activities of particular groups or cultures, but to contribute to the whole life of the variegated community. The community is now sufficiently mature for members of different religions to be able to share their faith with one another. For local Christians this is an exciting opportunity. Whereas in former days they used to contribute money to missionary organisations to send missionaries overseas, now the mission field has come to them, and they are able to share their faith with their neighbours in an ideal, relaxed and open manner. The Centre currently has seven different Christian congregations meeting on a Sunday, and numerous ethnic activities during the weekdays.

12.13 African Churches

The African churches in Britain are younger than the West Indian churches. They still have their first generation in leadership positions, and they are now contending with their second generation. They are beginning to recognise that their children, born in Britain, are now suffering from the pressures of living within two cultures where they are black on the outside and white inside. Their skin colour identifies them with the black migrant communities and in particular with the African groups to which their parents belong, but they identify with their white peer group with whom they are educated in school and mix in the local community. The Africans, however, have the advantage of mainly coming from the more privileged classes of Nigerian society who put great value on education. Most of them are economically advantaged in comparison with the first generation of West Indians, but there are lessons that the Africans need to learn from the experience of the West Indians who came mostly from the working classes in Jamaica and other Caribbean Islands.

A major problem which the African churches have yet to recognise is the elitism of their leadership that is rapidly becoming institutionalised. The West Indian churches in Britain have been successful in training working class leadership. Although they lost most of the second generation of the migrant population, their new generation of leadership has grown out of the working classes into a new professional class with an understanding of working class norms that is likely to reap an abundant harvest for good in the future.

By contrast, the African churches are at present steadily maintaining an elitist leadership with little understanding of the issues facing their own second generation in the migrant population. Unless they are able to bridge the gap with their second generation, and to develop leadership that is genuinely in touch with their grassroots communities, they are likely to repeat the experience of the West Indian churches and lose a whole generation.

This is a sociological situation which has been developing in Britain for several decades that is little short of tragic. There is a gulf between between the churches serving the African migrants in Britain and those serving the Caribbeans. The African churches began a period of rapid growth about the year 2000 and now have some of the largest congregations in Britain. Their total membership vastly outnumbers that of churches led by Caribbeans, although the latter churches are some fifty years older.

But the African churches are locked into a self-fulfilling mode whereby they are not looking for fellowship with others. They are single-minded in providing for the spiritual and social needs of Africans — mainly West Africans under Nigerian leadership. Their greatest need, although they are not yet aware of it, is to sit at the feet (or spiritually to wash the feet) of their brothers and sisters from the Caribbean, who have had fifty years' experience of coping with life in Britain. But for many Africans it would be unthinkable that they could learn anything from the descendants of slavery. The African migrants in Britain have no legacy of slavery. They were never captured in their home villages and deported across the Atlantic into slavery, and they are a proud people.

We have already noted in Chapter 6 how colonial slavery robbed the Caribbean Africans of their identity, blotting out their tribal roots, African names, language, culture, traditions and belief, and replacing them with a new identity as plantation chattel in total subjugation and submission to European authority. This taught them that they were a lesser species of humanity than the Europeans whom they were always to serve as their masters. The whole system for three hundred years enforced the mindset of slavery which, despite superficial changes to the system, takes many generations to remove. It institutionalises a fear of authority figures such as the police, government officials, social workers, teachers and other professional people. It is very difficult to de-mythologise this fear, even with education and upward social mobility.

12.14 An Illustration from History

The legacy of slavery is hard to eradicate. This is well illustrated in the history of the Hebrew people. They suffered four hundred years of slavery in Egypt. As each generation passed, the next generation, born into slavery, became more firmly institutionalised into a slave mentality. They were the children of slaves, and they had no social status or human rights. They were born to be under the authority of the masters who owned them and had total control of their lives from birth to death.

When they were released from slavery they spent forty years in the wilderness as an itinerant people, led by Moses *en route* to the land of promise. But the spirit of slavery was still in them and they had no confidence in their own ability to face strangers. An advance party sent ahead into the land of Canaan reported back that the people were giants. They said "*All the people who live there are powerful and the cities are fortified and very large.*" It was a Gentile named Caleb, who had gone with the explorers, who expressed a contrary view, saying, "*We should go up and take possession of the land, for we can certainly do it.*" He was overruled by the Hebrews in the advance party, who said: "*All the people we saw there are of great size. We seemed like grasshoppers in our own eyes, and we looked the same to them.*"[20]

The words "*We seemed like grasshoppers in our own eyes*" reveals the low self-esteem of the people, and this is reinforced by their perception of how they appeared in the eyes of others. It is interesting that the only man in the advance party who spoke out in favour of an immediate attack was Caleb, who came from a Gentile Edomite clan in the northern part of the Negev. We have no information on how he linked up with the Hebrews, but it is highly unlikely that he would have been part of the slave community in Egypt. The following day, Joshua, who later became Moses' successor, joined Caleb in saying that they should "*not be afraid of the people of the land*" but they should put their trust in God. The people, however, wailed "*Wouldn't it be better for us to go back to Egypt?*"[21]

The spirit of slavery was so strongly embedded in their psyche that they felt insecure and unable to accept the responsibility for their own destiny which their new freedom demanded — they would rather go back to the security of slavery in Egypt. They refused to accept Moses' leadership, which resulted in a whole generation dying in the wilderness. They had to wait for the next generation to have the courage to cross the Jordan under a new leader and re-enter the land their forefathers had left 400 years earlier.

12.15 The Spirit of Slavery

The spirit of slavery can be seen in attitudes among young people within the inner-city communities where gang life reproduces plantation life — where obedience to the gang leader is mandatory, and the authority he exercises is often brutal. The low self-esteem of the young people involved in gang life is vividly illustrated in black on black brutality. This is a form of self-harming, which is an extreme form of self-loathing and lack of self-esteem.

White boys in the inner-city communities suffer from a similar lack of self-esteem which is part of the legacy of white slavery dating back to the fatherless children of the Industrial Revolution who were raised in orphanage institutions until they were six or seven years of age when they were put (or sold) into apprenticeships, which was another form of slavery under cruel masters. That legacy of slavery continued for more than a hundred years in the bitter industrial relationships between workers and masters throughout the era of prosperity under Queen Victoria. The owners of industry were eventually forced to accept the existence of trade unions, but relationships between workers' unions and management are still not easy even today in the twenty-first century. There are, therefore, powerful forces of social control drawing together black and white boys in inner-city areas of Britain today, giving them a common heritage in a legacy of slavery that forms an underclass mindset.

12.16 Thinking outside the Box

Until there is recognition of the injustice suffered by former generations and the reality of the legacy that has been handed down through the generations, there will be no release for the victims. A sign of hope for the future lies with a growing movement among Christian leaders in the Caribbean communities in Britain who are keenly aware of the existence of the legacy of slavery among their own young people—and are beginning to articulate the phenomena associated with it — that has hitherto been unrecognised.

A small group of these Caribbean leaders willing to 'think outside the box' met in London in December 2013 to discuss what could be done about young people in inner-city areas of Britain. The Rev. Alton Bell, author of the book *Breaking the Chains of Mental Slavery*, voiced the feelings of many in saying that the enslavement of Africans in the Caribbean between the fifteenth and nineteenth centuries has had lasting effects which are at the root of some of the problems black people experience in twenty-first century society. The group recognised that, in the same way as South Africans linked truth and reconciliation, there has to be honesty and openness in facing the truth about the legacy of slavery that exists today among both black and white young people in some communities in British cities.

It may be unpleasant for some to face, but truth is needed if there are to be genuinely harmonious community relationships in multicultural Britain. And the truth is that all the people in the Caribbean islands, and their compatriots in Britain, are affected in some way by a legacy of slavery which is the result of three centuries of brutal British colonial policy, and it has never been acknowledged that the great wealth of British cities was accumulated out of the proceeds of oppression, and no steps have ever been taken towards acknowledging this colossal injustice.

12.17 Breaking the Yoke

In the Bible there is a significant verse in the history of the Hebrew people where God said to them through Moses their leader, "*I am the Lord your God, who brought you out of Egypt so that you would no longer be slaves to the Egyptians; I broke the bars of your yoke and enabled you to walk with heads held high*."[22] Maybe it is only God who can break the yoke of slavery through changing the mindset, attitudes and behaviour of those suffering from the legacy of slavery, but there is surely a great deal that can be done by those who recognise the injustices of the past. Churches in British cities working in inner-city areas could play a significant part in social transformation. Many are already doing excellent work among young people, often with limited resources. But so much more could be done with the right strategy and increased support. Many young people in inner-city and urban areas, both black and white, lack the opportunity to develop their natural gifts and abilities, which inevitably produces a sense of deprivation and frustration. They see themselves as victims of injustice and they feel unfulfilled.

12.18 Community Development

If churches would adopt 'community development' principles in their community activities, they could help to overcome the sense of powerlessness in society. Through 'community development' the natural abilities and gifts of individuals are identified so that they can be given opportunities to exercise and develop those gifts. The fact that somebody trusts them, and sees their potential, transforms attitudes and develops leadership skills. This is particularly necessary for both black and white young people in urban situations. Those inner-city churches that are doing sterling work should be recognised and encouraged by local authorities and national Government because they are able to reach into communities that are beyond the reach of many other institutions.

The New Testament Church of God, which works largely with the West Indian community, has an imaginative leadership training programme for pastors and key leaders. They say that their objective is to equip leaders to be intentionally inspirational and transformational in their practice and expectations. It is this kind of initiative that needs support and encouragement from the state.

But the work being done by the African and Caribbean churches, and their even greater potential is largely unrecognised and unsupported. They are simply left to struggle with their own very limited resources without even the backing or co-operation of the local white traditional churches. If the multiracial inner-city areas of British cities are to be transformed, and if we are not to have a repeat of the Tottenham Riots, then there are two essential developments that need to take place.

12.19 Essential Developments

The first essential is for the churches to repent of the separation between black and white Christians in the urban areas of British cities. It is surely a scandal that although Caribbean Christians and African Christians coming from similar denominational backgrounds have been resident in British cities for more than fifty years, there is still virtually a total separation between the traditional white British churches and the black-led Caribbean and African churches. In some places there are occasional inter-church meetings of leaders, but inter-church community activities are virtually unknown. If black and white churches cannot meet together to establish local Christian multicultural communities they cannot expect to have a role in the transformation of society.

In many towns and cities churches are working together to organise and run food banks and Street Pastors, both of which are meeting local needs and serving the community. But as far as I am aware no African churches and only one Caribbean church participates in this kind of activity. There is an urgent need for the black church leaders to review their mission and their outreach into the community.

The second essential is for statutory authorities to recognise the value of the contribution that Christian churches can make to the transformation of an area. In many places there are Christian organisations which are not church-based but are doing imaginative work with young people, such as XLP in south London, going into schools and dealing with the issues of guns, gangs and drugs. But programmes are also needed to work with parents. Investment with parents and infants would save the nation millions of pounds in future expenditure. Politicians seem to have dropped the whole concept of "Big Society" in which third sector or voluntary organisations play a central role in serving the community. But the churches have the potential to reach the unreached groups in many neighbourhoods if they had a joined-up strategy involving black and white churches in equal partnership with the recognition and cooperation of statutory authorities. They could be a significant force for the transformation of society.

12.20 The Denominational Churches

Looking back over many years, my greatest regret has been the lack of involvement of 'white'[23] churches from the earliest days of the migration. There were huge opportunities in the 1950s when churchgoing was at its height in the post-war period of reconstruction. In the early 1950s, when more than half of the nation's children went to Sunday School, every one of them had some biblical teaching in day school which at least gave them the basic values of corporate and personal morality which have formed the social foundations of the nation for centuries. This was a time when the biblical values of justice, equality and respecting one another in a multicultural society could (and should) have been established at every level in society.

Churches, which should have led the way by embracing the newcomers as brothers and sisters in Christ, neither opened their doors nor their arms to their new neighbours. The inner-city churches entered on a pathway of steep decline, and in a single decade (the 60s) church attendance dropped to a mere 0.5% in some inner-city areas. The churches rapidly lost the ability to reach the new multicultural urban masses.

They simply lost touch at one of the most crucial periods of social change in our history.

If there is any one group in society that should bear the greatest responsibility for allowing the creation of the 'communities of the dispossessed' in UK cities today it is the traditional denominational churches. This was more by neglect than deliberate policy. They did not become actively involved in the settlement of the migrant communities neither did they actively participate in the social and political arenas on behalf of the voiceless and the powerless in days of intense suffering. They did not follow basic Christian teaching in bearing the burdens of the poor or welcoming strangers. The churches were peacefully sleeping when the greatest movement of population in Britain for a thousand years took place. So the opportunity for creative involvement in a new kind of society was lost.

Jesus identified with the poor and the powerless as well as the sick and the outcast in society. Most of our churches did not. My own church in Tottenham was said to be the only fully multi-racial church in London at that time. If others had done the same it would have had an enormous impact upon the social environment in initiating both corporate and personal transformation. It could have changed the face of British cities.

The big question today is: can there be a second chance? I believe there can be if the Caribbean and African churches will come out of their social isolation and take their place in the forefront of a united move to transform social structures in the inner-city which will set young people free to develop their abilities and skills, releasing them from their present bondage; and if the traditional white churches will take their place alongside the black-led churches in a true partnership of equality dedicated to serving the local community and meeting their needs.

The black-led churches are the only institutions that can reach into some communities and they are now well established and have developed their own professional leadership. In many places they are stronger than the local white churches, but there has to be a determination on both sides for black and white to come together in partnership and mutual respect, to work together to transform our inner cities — and to ensure that the scourge of rioting never again takes place, and that the energy and creative ability of young people, both black and white, is rightly employed in building a better society in a safe, pleasant and healthy environment.

My first book, published in 1958, was called *Black and White in Harmony*. It seems strange to be ending this book, 56 years later, with the same plea for black and white to come together.

Notes

[1] See St John's Gospel, chapter 13.

[2] See chapter 5, section 5.9.

[3] Chapter 3, section 3.4.

[4] Luke 11:4.

[5] 1 Corinthians 13:5.

[6] See illustrated section.

[7] See chapter 5, section 5.3.

[8] Daniel Dorling, *Injustice: Why Social Inequality Persists*, The Policy Press, Bristol, 2012.

[9] *Ibid.*, p. 25.

[10] On p. 25 of a 400pp book.

[11] Owen Jones, *Chavs: the demonization of the working class*, Verso, London, 2012.

[12] Article in *The Times,* 21 February 2008.

[13] Article by George Monbiot in *The Guardian*, 24 May 2010.

[14] *Chavs*, *op. cit.,* pp. 182–183.

[15] *Ibid.*, p. 263.

[16] Richard Wilkinson with Kate Pickett, *The Spirit Level: why more equal societies almost always do better*, Allen Lane, London, 2009.

[17] Will Hutton, *Them and Us: Changing Britain – why we need a fair society*, Abacus, London, 2011.

[18] David Lammy, *Out of the Ashes*, Guardian Books, London, 2011.

[19] In November 2012 it celebrated its fortieth anniversary as a thriving Christian centre serving a multicultural community.

[20] Numbers 13:30–33.

[21] Numbers 14:3.

[22] Leviticus 26:13.

[23] The traditional denominational churches.

1. Sunday evening worship in High Cross Church Tottenham —
the largest multicultural congregation in London in the 1960s

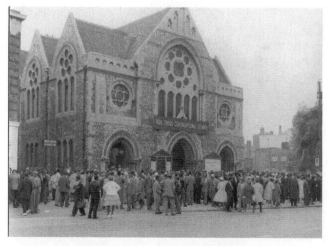

2. High Cross Church on Commonwealth Sunday 1963
— the church was full and latecomers were unable to gain entry

3. The church house attacked by the BNP July 1963
with Council workmen turning over the paving stones
to hide the offensive words NIGGER LOVER

4. The Zong slave ship moored in the Thames near Tower Pier
during the 200th anniversary commemorations of the
abolition of the slave trade, April 2007